Second Edition

PSYCHODYNAMIC COUNSELLING
in a nutshell

SAGE has been part of the global academic community since 1965, supporting high quality research and learning that transforms society and our understanding of individuals, groups and cultures. SAGE is the independent, innovative, natural home for authors, editors and societies who share our commitment and passion for the social sciences.

Find out more at: **www.sagepublications.com**

Susan Howard

Second Edition

PSYCHODYNAMIC COUNSELLING
in a nutshell

Los Angeles | London | New Delhi
Singapore | Washington DC

COUNSELLING IN A NUTSHELL SERIES Edited By Windy Dryden

© Susan Howard 2011

First published 2006. Reprinted in 2007, 2008 and 2009

This edition first published in 2011

Apart from any fair dealing for the purposes of research or private study, or criticism or review, as permitted under the Copyright, Designs and Patents Act, 1988, this publication may be reproduced, stored or transmitted in any form, or by any means, only with the prior permission in writing of the publishers, or in the case of reprographic reproduction, in accordance with the terms of licences issued by the Copyright Licensing Agency. Enquiries concerning reproduction outside those terms should be sent to the publishers.

SAGE Publications Ltd
1 Oliver's Yard
55 City Road
London EC1Y 1SP

SAGE Publications Inc.
2455 Teller Road
Thousand Oaks, California 91320

SAGE Publications India Pvt Ltd
B 1/I 1 Mohan Cooperative Industrial Area
Mathura Road
New Delhi 110 044

SAGE Publications Asia-Pacific Pte Ltd
33 Pekin Street #02-01
Far East Square
Singapore 048763

Library of Congress Control Number: 2010930982

British Library Cataloguing in Publication data

A catalogue record for this book is available from the British Library

ISBN 978-1-84920-745-4
ISBN 978-1-84920-746-1 (pbk)

Typeset by C&M Digitals (P) Ltd, Chennai, India
Printed in Great Britain by CPI Antony Rowe, Chippenham, Wiltshire
Printed on paper from sustainable resources

'The best simply got better. The first edition of this book was already quite simply the best introduction to psychoanalysis ever written and has been appropriately extremely popular with teachers and students alike. The thoroughly updated second edition retains all the powerful features of the first including its remarkable clarity and accessibility. It is like the homepage of Google, free of verbal clutter or jargon yet the interested reader will find most of what they need to know about what psychoanalysis is and what it is not, with ample links connecting to where to find the rest. This second edition includes plenty of new links to significant changes in the field, new areas that have emerged since the first edition and the most recent technical and clinical developments. The section on research in psychoanalysis is particularly helpful and it is reviewed like everything else in an amazingly accessible, balanced and entertaining way. There is no need to search any longer as to what to recommend to anyone who wants to orient themselves around this complex field. The field will be greatly indebted to these authors for many years.'

Professor Peter Fonagy, University College London

'This second edition draws you in and holds your attention from first page to last. The complexity of psychoanalysis is laid out before the reader with unsurpassed clarity. Comprehensive in its content yet concise in its delivery, a must read for those using psychoanalytic ideas in their professional practice or those with an academic or general interest.'

Martin Sheedy, Senior Lecturer and Social Work Programme leader, Centre for Social Work, Liverpool John Moores University

For Sarah and Oliver

Contents

Acknowledgements viii

1 Beginnings 1

2 Key Concepts in Psychodynamic Counselling 7

3 How Did We Get Here? 27

4 Putting Concepts into Practice: What Happens in Psychodynamic Counselling? 57

5 Practical Skills in Psychodynamic Counselling 71

6 Beyond Theory and Practice 85

Bibliography 105
Index 109

Acknowledgements

My particular thanks go to my husband, Peter, who once again has been generous in his support and encouragement of my writing endeavours. I also wish to thank Maureen Chapman, who has been my guide and tutor in understanding the modern Jungian position. Lastly, I would like to thank my editors, Alice Oven and Windy Dryden.

ONE

Beginnings

John had gone to his GP complaining of feeling low. His GP, who had known him for some time, felt that counselling might help and asked John to contact me. On first meeting him John did not give the impression of being obviously depressed. He was smartly dressed, cheerful and self-assured and, as he sat in the chair, he seemed to take up a lot of space in my room. He said he didn't quite know why he had come; he was sure he was wasting my time. I said that he was perhaps concerned that I wouldn't take his difficulties seriously. He looked relieved and said yes. I asked him what had taken him to his GP and he said that he had been feeling low and that he had been experiencing tightness in his chest. His GP had ruled out a physical cause for this and suggested that it might be the result of stress.

I asked him if he could identify anything that had caused him stress recently and he said he had been feeling low after a row with his wife, Anne. Following the row he had felt helpless and useless; the more he thought about the row the lower he felt. Eventually he had difficulties sleeping and was quite distracted at work. I said it sounded as though the row had upset him very much and asked him what it had been about. He told me that he had asked his wife to go on holiday with him to visit his cousin who was currently working in America. She had refused, saying that she had done all the travelling she wanted to do. Furthermore, Anne couldn't understand why he should want to go, since he had been before, and she made it clear that she would be very angry should he visit his cousin on his own.

'I'm not really that upset about it,' he said. 'I've been to America before and I don't need to go again. And anyway it would cost a lot of money, even if we did stay with my cousin.' He paused for a moment and then looked at me carefully and said, 'But every time I think about the row with Anne I get this tightening in my chest.' I said that it sounded as though Anne's refusal to visit America with him had upset him at a very profound level, to the extent that he could feel it in his body. He looked down at the carpet and was silent for a few minutes. I began to feel quite physically uncomfortable. I eventually realized that I felt as though I was suffocating. I decided to take the risk of reflecting my personal reaction to what John had told me and his own comment about the tightness in his chest and said, 'I wonder if the tightness in your chest makes you feel as though you are suffocating.' At this point he looked as though he might cry and began to tell me his story.

The story that unfolded was that Anne is 53 and 13 years older than John, who is nearly 40. They have been together for 14 years and married for 10. They have no children, though Anne has a daughter, Zoë, who is 33, from a previous marriage. John met Anne through his work – he is a supermarket manager and she had worked at a previous workplace as an administrator. At first they were very happy together, despite having to cope with a lot of disapproval from both their families because of the difference in their ages. Zoë had refused to speak to him for the first couple of years and John's older sister, Katherine, and his parents made their disapproval obvious too. Their fight against their respective families had brought them closer together, and for the first seven years of their marriage he had had no regrets.

'The problem is that once Anne turned 50 she suddenly seemed to change. All she talked about was retirement. She didn't want to work full-time any more, even though we still really needed the money for the mortgage. And now she intends to retire when she's 55,' he said. 'What's more, her friends just talk about retirement too. I'd never noticed the age difference before, but for the last three years it seems like we live in different worlds. I'm not ready to think about stopping work – I'm not 40 yet. The visit to America was the last straw. It seems like she's just resigned to sitting at home and she wants me to do the same. I want to go, but I know she'll just make life impossible if I do. And yes, I do feel suffocated.'

Later in the session John told me that he had once tried to talk to Anne about how he felt about their lives together. She had been angry with him, and said if that was how he felt he should go now. He became very upset, and shortly after became physically ill, necessitating a period of time off

> work. Anne cared for him through his illness and he thought about how difficult it would have been to look after himself if he had been alone. He had decided that he would not upset her again by complaining.

The way I related to John, the questions I asked and the sense I made of his answers was largely shaped by the model of counselling I have been trained in and use. Like the other models described in this series,[1] the psychodynamic model has assumptions or ideas implicit to it about how our minds work, how we develop psychologically, how we function emotionally, what causes emotional problems and therefore which counselling techniques will bring about psychological change.

The ideas that underpin each counselling model have a profound effect on the techniques we develop and the way we actually 'do' counselling. The model a counsellor uses will even affect what she[2] considers important in what her clients say to her. For example, my first comment to John was that I wondered whether he was afraid I'd take his concerns seriously. Using another model I might not have chosen to address the issue at all, or I might have addressed it more directly by reassuring him that I would take him seriously. But by saying that I wondered if he felt that I might *not* take him seriously I straightaway conveyed several things to him. The first was that it was all right to acknowledge how he was feeling at that moment – that he might be anxious about coming to counselling and fear that I might not understand his distress. Secondly, I wished to signal the opening up of an area that could be thought about, rather than closing down discussion, as I would have if I had reassured him that he need not be anxious. Lastly, that thinking about the relationship between us is a legitimate and central area for discussion in the work we will do together.

In conveying these thoughts I was already giving John an experience of some of the elements of psychodynamic work. I was indicating that I took his inner feelings seriously; I was demonstrating that exploration of thoughts and feelings was meaningful and that in counselling finding a space in which to think was important. In particular I was, from the very beginning of our work together, indicating to him that the relationship between us was central. Psychodynamic work emphasizes the importance of the relationship between practitioner and client in a way that is different from other models of counselling. Nearly all forms of therapeutic work pay attention to the importance of there being a good working relationship between client and counsellor. Some, for example Interpersonal Psychotherapy (IPT), acknowledge that the way a client experiences his counsellor and the kind of relationship he develops with her gives important information about other important relationships in his life. But it is the psychodynamic model that uniquely goes beyond this and says that the relationship between client and counsellor is, additionally, the central vehicle through which psychological change occurs.

> At the end of the first session I asked John if he wanted to come back to continue our conversation. When he said yes I asked what he hoped to gain from counselling. Initially he seemed surprised by the question, but then he said, 'I want the pain to go away.' I asked him which pain, and he replied that he wanted the chest pain to stop and then he added that he wanted to stop feeling low. In this way John conveyed to me that he was aware that his pain was not just physical, but emotional too. He also, I think, demonstrated some awareness of the fact that there could be a link between the two.

At this stage in his counselling John knew very little about psychodynamic counselling, what he might expect and whether this was the best approach for him. In reality he therefore did not know what he was agreeing to in saying he would come back to continue our conversation. Practitioners in other therapeutic models may at this stage endeavour to obtain formal informed consent from their client before proceeding further. By informed consent I mean that the client has sufficient relevant information about counselling to understand what he is agreeing to, including the nature, risks and benefits of the approach and the alternative approaches available. In common with many other psychodynamic practitioners I have not sought to gain informed consent at this stage and have done so for a number of reasons.

The major difficulty lies in the fact that until John has some experience of psychodynamic counselling he will be unable to know what he is consenting to. I could explain something of the nature of psychodynamic counselling to him, but it would probably not mean very much outside the context of experiencing it. Consent given at this stage may therefore not be truly 'informed'. At the same time there is a tension between giving John enough information to enable him to make an informed choice about continuing while not disrupting the nascent therapeutic relationship between us which will allow the emergence of unconscious material. As I said previously, the therapeutic relationship is the central vehicle through which therapeutic change occurs, so my first task is to facilitate the development of that relationship. Often people in great distress do not want to hear about the advantages and disadvantages of a particular approach. They want their distress to be heard and taken seriously. Not to do so may inhibit the development of the relationship if the client feels that the counsellor is more concerned with her own agenda (to discuss risks and benefits) than his. Having said this, should a client ask about the nature, risks and benefits of counselling or other counselling approaches in the very early sessions, it should be discussed.

Obtaining informed consent as soon as is practicable is a matter of good practice and I will need to address the issue with John at some point near the beginning of his counselling. The question is when? One way is to make a distinction between the assessment and 'treatment' phases of counselling, and to discuss consent at the end of an assessment phase once John has had some experience of the approach so that he better understands what he is consenting to. To some extent, making a distinction between assessment and treatment creates an artificial division, since psychodynamic practitioners argue that assessment is continuous and treatment begins the moment a client makes contact. However, it may be helpful to organize one's thinking around this division for the purpose of gaining informed consent.

Not to gain his explicit consent means that I have assumed that John has given implicit consent to counselling by virtue of coming to see me. However, there are dangers in this, the most important of which is that John is vulnerable to commencing counselling without understanding the potential risks or difficulties involved. For example, many people who enter psychodynamic counselling find their relationships with important others in their lives change as they change, and this is likely to be true for John. Almost always this is generally for the better, but these changes can also involve losing friends or even a partner where the relationship has contributed to the emergence or maintenance of a client's distress. It is important that John understands these risks before he becomes too involved in the process of counselling.

We will return to John throughout the book and link his progress through counselling. I will use additional case material as well. In the next chapter I have set out some of the concepts that define the psychodynamic model and set it apart from other models of counselling. Chapter 3 is an exploration of the theory behind the practical skills, which describes why we do what we do. In Chapter 4, I will look at what actually happens in psychodynamic counselling, from the perspective of both counsellor and client. In Chapter 5, I describe some of the practical skills involved in psychodynamic counselling. Lastly, in Chapter 6, I will be looking at the context in which psychodynamic counselling takes place, including the evidence base for this approach.

Notes

1 I have omitted making references in the text. Instead I have listed further reading in the Bibliography at the back of the book.
2 For the sake of clarity, I will refer to the counsellor as 'she' and the client as 'he' throughout, except when describing specific case studies.

TWO

Key Concepts in Psychodynamic Counselling

Watching counsellors trained in other models at work has helped me realize that the way we do counselling is largely determined by the model we work within. From the most fundamental aspects of the relationship, such as how we greet a client, to the use of advanced therapeutic skills like making interpretations, our whole way of relating to and thinking about our client is driven by the theoretical model we subscribe to. It is therefore important to know what it is that defines the model we use and what differentiates one model from the other. This then allows us to have an understanding of why we do what we do.

The psychodynamic model

First of all, I should make it clear that there is no such thing as '*The* Psychodynamic Model'. 'Psychodynamic' is an umbrella term that refers to all models of the mind that are primarily concerned with unconscious processes. All psychodynamic models (and a number of models, like Cognitive Behavioural Therapy (CBT) that now have no allegiance to psychoanalytic thinking) trace their lineage back to Freud and psychoanalysis. Psychoanalysis remains the most influential of the psychodynamic models, though some thinkers like Jung, Adler and Reich developed Freud's ideas in such different directions that they founded separate schools of psychodynamic thinking.

Modern psychoanalytic thinking has not remained the same as it was in Freud's day, however. Just as in other intellectual and scientific disciplines, the important thinkers within psychoanalysis since Freud have revised and developed his theories in the light of experience and research. At the same time they acknowledge that some of what he said remains relevant today. Much of what I describe below is found in all psychodynamic models, but where there are differences between the models I will privilege the psychoanalytic model for the sake of clarity.

We all have an unconscious inner world

Psychodynamic models take as their starting point the proposition that we have an 'inner world' that has a powerful influence on how we think, feel and behave. Our inner world is comprised of feelings, memories, beliefs and fantasies. It is partly conscious, meaning that we know about it and have access to it. But it is largely unconscious, meaning that we are by definition unaware of it and do not have access so easily. In the recent past the notion of the existence of an unconscious mind was itself controversial, particularly in mainstream psychology. However, today advances in neuroscience have brought the unconscious into mainstream psychology and unconscious awareness is recognized in many cognitive psychological theories, including theories of perception and learning, though the terminology used can be different.

Freud believed he had evidence that the unconscious mind follows a different set of rules from our conscious mind. He argued that unconscious mental life is governed by primary processes, whereas conscious mental life is governed by secondary mental processes. By this he meant that the conscious mind is organized according to the rules of logic, is in touch with reality, can defer gratification and understands concepts of time and the difference between things and people. By contrast, primary or unconscious processes are not constrained by reality. Time can collapse, so that an event that happened many years ago can be experienced as though it is happening in the present. Contradictions can exist within primary process thinking and one thing can stand for another, for example a snake might not just represent a penis (as it would in secondary process thinking) but *become* one. Freud also believed that the unconscious mind is governed by the 'pleasure principle', meaning that it demands immediate gratification of instinctual pleasures and is motivated to get those pleasures met.

It is possible to think of gradations of consciousness, so that some parts of our unconscious mind are more readily accessible than others. One of the aims of psychodynamic counselling is to make more of our minds available to conscious awareness, so that we can live our lives more aware of what motivates us and therefore have more freedom and choice about how we act. However, we can never be fully aware, rather just better at working out what might be going on. Our unconscious can, however, be inferred by ourselves and by other people, for example, by how we behave, the things we say or feelings we experience. More specifically it can be worked out through the stories we tell, the dreams we relate and other 'give-aways' such as jokes, slips of the tongue and the use of metaphor and symbolism.

Freud was particularly interested in how our unconscious can be seen in everyday life. He felt that the interpretation of dreams was 'the royal road' to a knowledge of the unconscious. Through analysis of dreams Freud believed he could elucidate the workings of the unconscious mind, particularly by revealing wishes, fears or conflicts that the conscious mind could not tolerate. He distinguished between what he called the manifest content (the actual story) and the latent content (the hidden story) of dreams. He argued that the manifest content and meaning of the dream both represent and disguise the hidden 'story' and meaning. He believed that the latent content was usually to do with forbidden sexual or aggressive wishes and therefore too anxiety-provoking to be directly represented in the dream. Today we don't limit our understanding of dreams to representing only sexual or aggressive anxieties and wishes. Instead we look to dreams to help us understand how the dreamer relates to other important people in his world.

10 Psychodynamic Counselling in a Nutshell

> In his second session with me John said he had had a dream the previous night that had disturbed him, though he didn't understand why. He described how he was in his car with a female friend whom he'd only met recently, and they were setting out on a trip to an as yet undisclosed destination. They pulled into a service station to get fuel, and when he went to pay the cashier, she told him that his card was no longer valid as it had reached its credit limit. When he tried to explain to his friend that he could not afford to pay for the fuel she became very angry with him and said she wasn't going to go with him if he couldn't afford the trip. He was very upset and didn't know what to do. At that point his mother appeared and said he should come home with her as his dinner was waiting and they were going out together that evening.
>
> When I asked John what he thought about the dream he said that he had, in fact, lost his credit card at a service station the day before the dream. He had been worried that his wife would be angry with him, but she had been very understanding about it. He then remembered that in the dream his mother had been wearing his wife's favourite hat.

The manifest content of this dream is about a car journey that is cut short because John could not pay for the fuel. His new friend was unsympathetic, but his mother rescued him and told him to come home. The dream is built around actual events that had happened recently, what Freud termed the 'day residue'.

It is not uncommon for clients at the beginning of counselling to have dreams about going on a journey, which is often understood as a dream about the start of the therapeutic journey. Quite often these dreams are infused with anxiety about the forthcoming journey, even though consciously the client might say he is looking forward to starting counselling.

In his dream John was going on the journey with a new friend, which I understood as a representation of me. But he was unable to pay for the journey. John had some concerns about the financial cost of counselling, but his anxiety in the dream was more likely to be about how much it would cost him in other respects. By this I mean that unconsciously John was probably anxious about the emotional cost to him of starting counselling, about what he might find out about himself and what he might reveal to me. He would be facing up to painful issues and his life might well change as a result in ways that he had not yet imagined. In the dream, when he couldn't afford the cost of the journey, I became angry and wouldn't continue the journey with him. I wondered about the extent to which, at an unconscious level, he already experienced me as unsympathetic to any difficulties he might have in managing the emotional cost of his counselling. Lastly, and importantly, his mother comes and rescues him from the difficult situation he is in, and I wondered about whether she represented his wife. The clue lies in her wearing his wife's hat. The dream may therefore tell us something about the nature of John's relationship with his wife, and the extent to which she represents his mother in his internal world. It also points to the possibility of a conflict between a part of him that wants to escape from his wife and the part of him that fears he cannot succeed in doing so and remains dependent on her.

Freud also argued that we often reveal what our true, but unconscious, wishes or conflicts are through jokes, or slips of the tongue. Most of us are aware of the cruelty or anger that can often underlie a joke, but which it can be difficult to confront. Or we know people who say very contentious or aggressive things and then say, 'I was just joking'. At some level we are usually aware of the hidden attack implicit in these jokes, though the teller himself may not be conscious of it. Likewise slips of the tongue can reveal motives or wishes that we have hidden from other people or ourselves.

Psychodynamic practitioners today also talk about our inner world (conscious and unconscious) being populated by the important people in our lives, like parents or other carers, or a partner. These people are known in psychodynamic terminology as 'objects' and our relationship with them as 'object relationships'. This rather unfortunate terminology came about because Freud, who first described the concept, wrote in German, which was sometimes translated in a way that lost the subtlety of some of its original meaning. Object relationships are understood as being the product of both the actual relationship with carers and the distortions of that relationship brought about by unconscious fantasy. Understanding and elucidating a person's object relationships tells us much about how he experienced his early relationships, though because actual experience was distorted by fantasy they can only tell us a limited amount about what actually went on.

In common with counsellors practising in other models, psychodynamic counsellors work with conscious aspects of their clients' inner worlds to bring about psychological change. This is a very important aspect of all counsellors' work, whatever their model. However, what makes the psychodynamic model distinct from other models is that it emphasizes the importance of the unconscious mental life of our clients. Translated into practice, psychodynamic counsellors seek to help their clients become aware of their inner world, and to make conscious and explicit as much as possible of the mind's workings that were previously unconscious and implicit.

Our inner world is dynamic

A basic proposition that sets the psychodynamic model apart from other models is that the unconscious is dynamic, and therefore purposeful. Consequently, it is a source of motivation for our behaviour, feelings and fantasies, rather than just something we are unaware of. Although mainstream psychology and psychodynamic psychology now agree about the existence of the unconscious, there remains a disagreement between them regarding whether or not it is dynamic and therefore an important source of motivation.

Quite often people believe that as we are unaware of what is going on in our unconscious inner world, it has no effect on us. However, psychodynamic models hold that it is often unconscious memories, needs, feelings and fantasies that have the most profound effect on the way that we experience the world around us. Furthermore, our actions and conscious beliefs are largely driven by our attempts to keep uncomfortable truths from our conscious awareness. This in itself is an extremely uncomfortable proposition as it means that we are not totally in charge of our feelings or behaviour. As a species we have a tendency to think we can control most things, and this belief is supported by advances in science and technology.

So a model that takes as its central premise that we are not totally in control is very threatening to many. But there are many everyday examples of how our unconscious mind takes precedence over our conscious mind. For example, how often do we find ourselves repeating destructive behaviours that we promised ourselves we would never do again, and really not understand why we are doing so? The psychodynamic model accounts for this by saying that our unconscious motivation to repeat the destructive behaviour takes precedence over our conscious motivation not to. It then seeks to understand what that unconscious motivation might be.

The word 'dynamic' refers to movement, or turbulence, meaning that our inner world is not static, but always changing. Turbulence is seen as a normal aspect of psychological functioning, since the world we live in is constantly changing and we have to adapt to those changes. The strength and amount of turbulence varies, however, according to how much pressure we are under at any given moment. The pressure can come from internal or external sources. By internal sources I mean instinctual needs (see below), memories, fantasies, beliefs and wishes; also our relationship to ourselves and important others in our minds. By external sources I mean events or relationships in the outer world that affect us. My image of my own internal world is that it is like a 'lava' lamp in which coloured convection currents are in perpetual and ever-changing movement in relation to one another. The amount of movement in the lamp is determined by the amount of heat in the system. In a similar way the amount of turbulence there is in our inner world is determined by the amount of psychological 'heat' being generated by pressure from inside us (our inner world) or from the external world. John came to counselling at a time when the amount of psychological turbulence he was experiencing had increased to the point where it was causing considerable discomfort and he could no longer cope with it on his own.

We all experience inner conflict

Very often we experience these convection currents as a clash or a conflict, and this notion of conflict and the pain it can cause is also a central idea in the psychodynamic model. The psychodynamic model views the experience of being human as an inherently uncomfortable one. We constantly have to reconcile the tension between the things we want for ourselves, the demands of living in groups with others and what, in reality, is possible. We have to make ongoing adjustments and compromises to changes in our external world. And this is not the only compromise we have to make. We also have our own set of internal guiding principles about how we should live life. So we cannot do what we want when we want. If we do not obey society's rules and our own conscience we will pay a price. So we cannot drive as fast as we want, take things that belong to other people, hurt them if they get in our way and so on. Sometimes we want to do these things very much, and when the wish to do so is powerful it can be very distressing and difficult to cope with.

In his conscious mind John was aware of the conflict between his wish to have more variety and interest in his life and his fear that should he go to America Anne would punish him. However, the conscious manifestation of the conflict may also overlie a wish to leave Anne while being afraid of the humiliation of being seen to have made a mistake in marrying her. At present this conflict is probably preconscious, in other words not that far below conscious awareness and therefore not too difficult to get to. At a deeper level of his unconscious mind there will be other conflicts to do with John's relationship with Anne, who she represents to him unconsciously and how he sees himself in his own mind.

The psychodynamic model seeks to account for John's feeling of suffocation through understanding first its conscious aspects and then the unconscious distress underlying it. It involves helping him to become consciously aware of underlying conflict and helping him to tolerate the pain that is inevitable when he faces it.

We all need psychological defences

This brings me to the next important idea in the psychodynamic model, which is that we need to find ways of coping with the inherent discomfort of the human condition and the conflict it causes, so that

Key Concepts in Psychodynamic Counselling   15

we are not overwhelmed. The ways we have of coping are called 'defences'. We can use psychological defences quite consciously and deliberately, but the psychodynamic model is particularly interested in those defences that we deploy unconsciously. Freud saw 'repression', a form of forgetting, as particularly significant. This he understood as a way of making, and then keeping, unconscious any wishes or thoughts that are threatening and may therefore become a source of anxiety. He saw the aim of psychoanalytic work as making the unconscious conscious through lifting repression. Modern psychodynamic thinkers also acknowledge the importance of repression, but they don't place it as centrally as Freud did.

John indicated that one of his mechanisms of protecting himself is a defence known as 'denial', which means that we deny the fact that something is upsetting us in order not to have to be distressed about what we can't have. John also used 'rationalization', which is a defence whereby we give ourselves a rational and reasonable story to account for or justify something that is uncomfortable. John used both defences in talking about his disappointment about his trip to America. At first he denied that he minded not going; then he said that he'd already been to America and didn't need to go again; that he couldn't afford it anyway. By doing this he aims not to feel so badly about his disappointment. However, his defences are not working very well, as he quickly tells me that he gets a pain in his chest every time he thinks about the row with Anne. This time John's defences are operating at an almost conscious level. It would not, therefore, come as too great a shock should I point out to him how he is trying to fend off his disappointment.

We develop defences early in life in order to manage the challenges of coping with the inevitable discomfort of being human. Very often people enter counselling at a time when their defences are no longer serving them well. They are either too rigid and make life difficult (for example, the person who uses denial to the point he no longer faces any problem), or they might have collapsed altogether (for example, the person who cannot get out of bed for fear of something terrible happening). We need defences to be able to function in the world, so it is not the aim of psychodynamic work to eliminate them. That would not only be unwise, but impossible. At the same time we need our defences to be sufficiently flexible that they allow us to respond according to the particular situation we are in, rather than treating all situations as though they were the same. Defences applied rigidly are unhelpful, because they reduce the choices we have about how we respond, and we are likely to find ourselves in even greater difficulty because we have reacted inappropriately. The vignette below demonstrates how a defence can get in the way of real understanding when it is applied rigidly.

> Stella found it difficult to be a client. She was frightened that if she became vulnerable and allowed me close to her I would in some way damage her. One day she was talking about her parents, with whom she had had a difficult and painful early relationship: 'Giving up the hatred of one's parents is an ideal theoretical position, but the concept of acceptance is partial.' Her highly technical language in one way described her dilemma about the pain involved in realizing that she could not let go of her hatred for her parents. She often used the defence of intellectualization as a way of keeping both me and her own feelings at a distance. At this level her defence had worked as she was succeeding in cutting out me, as well as her own feelings.

Defences become part of the very structure of our character, and are an important determinant of our personal style in the way we relate to the world. Very often psychodynamic texts give long lists of defences, including the ones I have described above. However, modern psychodynamic thinking is less mechanistic and tends to look at how we can use any experience or feeling in a defensive way. Nevertheless, there are two more defences that I think it is important to describe as they are commonly observed in everyday life and frequently experienced in the consulting room. The first is projection and the second is splitting.

Projection is the means by which we attribute to other people characteristics in ourselves that are unacceptable to us. Like other defences, projection operates at an unconscious level, so we are unaware that we are doing it, though sometimes we can feel uncomfortable when we have attacked someone for having a characteristic we have projected into them.

> Jeremy was an extremely caring man, and was often selfless in his relationships to others. In counselling it became clear, however, that he was secretly very critical of those he considered selfish. His stories were often about those whose behaviour he condemned for their self-centredness, and at times he hinted that I too was selfish and put my needs before those of my clients. I hypothesized to myself that he felt unconscious anxiety about his own selfishness and that he resolved this by projecting it into those around him.

One of the goals of psychodynamic work is to help the client to recognize what he has projected and to accept it as a part of him. The process of taking back projections and owning them is called 'reintrojection'. In this case, Jeremy needed help to recognize the extent to which he was selfish, and how that impacted on his relationships with others. It also involved exploring the anxiety behind what it means to be selfish. Jeremy feared that if he gave full rein to his selfishness he would become unlovable and alienate those on whom he depended.

In order to project an unwanted part of us into someone else we have to first split that part off from conscious awareness. Splitting occurs when it is psychologically too threatening to hold two things together at the same time, for example to see oneself as both selfish and caring. Human beings have a strong tendency to split things into opposites and only see one aspect of a complex situation. In particular, we tend to see others or ourselves as all good or all bad. It is a sign of psychological maturity when we can mange the tensions involved in bringing opposites together, for example being able to acknowledge that we can love and hate the same person.

Psychological symptoms are rooted in our inner world

The psychodynamic model holds that psychological symptoms are the external expression of distress in our internal world. This may be the result of developmental difficulties in our early lives (for example early neglect or trauma) or internal conflict (for example between competing wishes or needs). An example of a developmental difficulty leading to symptoms is someone who, as a baby, was left to cry alone for long periods of time. Because their carer did not reliably help them with their distress, they would not have internalized an experience of being helped and therefore may not have the internal resources to manage later distress. As an adult that person might become very anxious, though it might be difficult for them to understand why. Psychodynamic theory holds that the underlying need to feel safe needs to be addressed in counselling and that once the person has an experience of being safely held by their counsellor they will become more able to hold their own distress and the symptoms of anxiety will reduce. Although psychodynamic practitioners acknowledge that treatments that just focus on treating symptoms can make a difference in the short term, they maintain that unless the underlying cause is worked with the symptoms are likely to return. This is particularly the case when the developmental needs or inner conflict underlying the symptoms are still creating turbulence.

Symptoms are seen as both an expression of distress and, sometimes, as also symbolizing that distress. For example, someone who cuts himself may be doing so in order to feel the pain associated with self harm because he is emotionally numb and he wants to be able to feel the pain he is in. In this case the symptom may give us a direct clue about the problem the client is presenting with.

We are motivated by our instincts

As human beings have become more sophisticated we have found it increasingly difficult to accept that we could be motivated by instincts in the same way other animals are. We like to think we are in charge of ourselves and that we know exactly what motivates us; that we are logical and rational and understand why we do what we do. Once again, psychodynamic theorists occupy an uncomfortable position as we *do* accept the proposition that we are not entirely in control. Psychodynamic theorists know that our instinctual needs can powerfully over-ride other, more 'civilized', behaviour. When this happens we can sometimes feel very badly about our resultant behaviour. As I was thinking about this section of the chapter I listened to a radio programme in which a woman described how she survived an air crash by climbing over other people to get out of the burning plane. Her instinct to survive was so powerful that she performed a physical feat that she would normally be unable to manage. However, ever since she has lived with guilt that her instinctual act of self-preservation allowed her to live when many others died.

Freud argued that the most important of the instincts is our sexual drive and that much of the reason for having psychological defences is to keep awareness of our sexual instincts from conscious awareness. Jung, however, was more aware of the importance of relationships and most psychodynamic thinkers today agree that our most basic instinctual need is to relate to other people. From the moment of birth we seek out relationships in whatever way we are able according to our level of maturation; our survival depends on our ability to relate to others and we are programmed to do so. At the same time neuroscientists have identified a number of 'instinctual circuits' that are common to all mammals, including man, and which reside in the primitive part of the brain. These circuits map on to and extend some of the instincts identified by Freud, such as the sexual drive, and confirm Freud's proposition that quite a lot of our behaviour is governed by our instincts.

Early childhood experiences influence our adult personality

There have been many times when I have suggested a link between a client's childhood experience and his current difficulties and I have received the surprised reply, 'But I can't remember much about my childhood' or 'That was a long time ago. It has nothing to do with what's happening now.' And, indeed, it is very difficult for that person to *feel* that there is a link. How can it be that things we don't even remember have a profound and lasting influence on the adults we become? Starting with Freud, psychodynamic theory has argued that early experience is a significant ingredient in determining both adult personality and later psychological difficulties. Again, this can be a very uncomfortable proposition. If someone has had a painful childhood he generally prefers to think that once he is an adult he will be able to determine who he is and that life will be better. He would rather not think that his childhood experience could make it difficult for him to cope with his adult life. It seems doubly unfair.

There has been a longstanding, and sometimes bitter, debate within psychodynamic thinking about the relative contribution of a child's fantasy world in the later development of his adult personality, and his actual experience of the world around him. On one side some theoreticians have argued that unconscious fantasy shapes our experience and is relatively more important than actual experience (see Chapter 3). On the other side of the debate there are those who argue that fantasy is shaped by the experience we have as children, and that it plays an important, but secondary, role in character formation. What has never been in dispute, however, is that childhood experience influences our adult personality. Psychodynamic psychology has always been rooted in developmental theory, and has sought to explain both our adult personalities and our psychological difficulties in relation to our developmental history.

We have a number of different memory systems. One, called episodic memory, is the system that remembers events. Few of us have memories of events much before our third birthday, and it is not uncommon for memory for events to start at around the age of five. Freud called this lack of early memory for events 'infantile amnesia' and thought it was the result of repression. However, we now know it is because the brain is not completely myelinated until we are about three, and myelination is needed in order for episodic memory to be laid down. So not remembering much before we are five or so is quite usual. However, clients who cannot remember much of their childhood after the age of five are understood as needing to forget and such a lack of memory suggests either that the client's childhood has been difficult, or there has been a trauma that he has coped with by forgetting everything that went before. Very early in my career I worked with a young woman who could remember nothing before the death of her mother when she was 10. The only way she could cope with the magnitude of her loss was to wipe out all memory of her mother and, since her mother was so central to my client's life, she forgot everything else before she was 10 as well.

However, another kind of memory, called implicit memory, begins to operate from when we are very tiny. This kind of memory is to do with learning skills and how to 'be with' others. We cannot remember learning to walk, but that knowledge is laid down in our implicit memory. Psychodynamic practitioners often talk about 'body memory' which is to do with our early experience of being handled by our carers and how the nature of that care is 'remembered' and emerges later in life by the way we care for ourselves.

Psychodynamic practitioners are interested in the early history of their clients so that they can understand the origins of their difficulties. Knowledge of a client's early history helps the counsellor to tailor her interventions to address the source of his problems. For example, in an earlier section of this chapter I talked about the experience of inner conflict and how that impacts on our psychological well-being. Some clients have experienced significant disruptions in their early relationships, or have a history of cruelty, neglect or trauma. Although they experience conflict, their more significant difficulty might lie in lacking a sense of who they are. In psychodynamic language we talk about the strength of their ego having being undermined by their experiences so that they have been unable to develop a robust sense of self. Consequently, their sense of identity can easily be destabilized. When such clients seek counselling their need for help initially lies in repairing these deficits rather than coping with the internal conflicts I referred to earlier.

Recent and exciting advances in neuroscience are beginning to support what psychodynamic clinicians have always argued. There is increasing evidence that our brains are sculpted by the emotional experiences we have from infancy – some even before we were born. Our early experiences with our carers interact with our genetic make-up to determine how our brains develop. For example, infants brought up in circumstances where they were frequently stressed experience high levels of cortisol in the brain, which impacts on how they react to stressful situations later in life. The long-term implication of this experience-driven development is that our behaviour as adults and our capacity to relate to others has a direct connection to our early experiences.

The relationship with a counsellor is central to change

The next tenet of the psychodynamic model holds that psychological change is brought about by the relationship between the client and his counsellor. There are three important elements to this relationship: the transference, the countertransference and the real relationship. Transference is the process by which the inner world of the client becomes revealed in counselling through the relationship he develops with his counsellor. This happens when we 'transfer' onto the relationship with a counsellor our expectations about how we will behave with or experience other people and how they will behave with or experience us. These expectations are created by our experience in reality or fantasy of our objects (carers, siblings or other important people) as children. Our early relationships thus become the template for our expectations of later relationships. We are quite active in attempting to re-create new object relationships that will fit the template of our previous experience, including those with our counsellor. Counsellors become transference objects for their clients partly because the counselling relationship is an intimate one that evokes memories of other intimate relationships. Also, coming into counselling leads to a degree of regression in the client because he has had to ask for help with a problem he cannot solve on his own, which puts him more forcefully in touch with earlier patterns of relating when he was dependent on his carers.

Complementary to the client's transference to his counsellor is the counsellor's countertransference to her client. By this I mean that the counsellor may become aware of feelings within herself that have arisen in response to her client's unconscious communication or state of mind. For example, a client may talk about an area of his life as though it was something that did not bother him, yet the counsellor may experience powerful feelings such as anger or sadness in response to the story, which may indicate that the client himself is unable to bear his own feelings of sadness or anger. Countertransference has become a vital tool in psychodynamic practice. It is now understood as an important source of communication from the client about states of mind that may not otherwise be available to expression.

The real relationship involves that part of the relationship which is relatively free of transference dynamics, so that it is more based in reality and is to do with two human beings connecting with one-another. Psychodynamic schools differ in the extent to which they accept the idea that the counselling relationship can ever be free of transference distortions, but in my own view clients' accurate perceptions of us are important to acknowledge, since they help orient them to reality. Also real things happen between counsellor and client during the course of their work together. The counsellor may have to cancel sessions at short notice, or she may be visibly unwell or upset. Acknowledging the accuracy of a client's perceptions at such a time can help him discover his counsellor as a new rather than a transferential object. Not to do so may impair his trust in his counsellor and his capacity to make the distinction between his internal and external worlds, which is one of the aims of psychodynamic counselling.

Receiving a client's unconscious communication can put a great deal of pressure on the counsellor, who might find herself experiencing unbearable feelings or wishing to act in ways that are unhelpful to her client. Sometimes the pressure to respond in a way that fits her client's template can result in the counsellor feeling, and even behaving, in accordance with the client's transferential expectations.

> As I got to know him better I realized that John's relationship with his objects was characterized by a combination of hostility and dependence. This was particularly evident in his relationship with Anne. On the one hand he was quite contemptuous of her and seemed to take pleasure in hurting her by rejecting her attempts to repair their relationship.

> He seemed unwilling to acknowledge how important she was to him. At the same time he was dependent on her in order to maintain a sense of internal equilibrium. Without her he would have found it very difficult to face the outside world, so he was careful not to push her too far away for fear of losing her altogether. In the relationship with me he was reluctant to acknowledge that I was helpful or important to him. In the countertransference I began to struggle with feeling that it didn't matter whether I worked hard in his sessions, as I felt that he didn't value me or the work I was doing with him. Yet at the same time he was meticulous about attending his sessions, and was rarely late or absent, despite a difficult journey and heavy work demands, indicating that the work we were doing together was important to him.
>
> John's transference to me also reflected his childhood experiences with his parents, particularly his mother. When he was a child, John's parents had a troubled relationship and his mother had recruited him as an ally against his father. He experienced his mother as intrusive and demanding and he was secretly contemptuous of her need of him. Yet at the same time he was quite excited by her and had felt special when she treated him as a confidant and more important than his father. Marrying Anne was the only time he overtly went against his mother's wishes and as an adult he continued to attempt to please her, even though he still complained about her intrusiveness. I began to hypothesize that in his relationship to me he was also caught between wanting to be special and needed, and fearing an intrusive closeness that might be too uncomfortable and arouse unwelcome feelings and fantasies.

By understanding the nature of our client's transference and our own countertransference we begin to understand something about what is going on in the client's inner world. He is telling us a little about how he experienced his early relationships and the behaviours, emotions and fantasies that dominate his current relationships. This is why the psychodynamic model places the relationship between a client and his counsellor at the centre of the work. It goes beyond recognizing how necessary it is that client and counsellor develop a good working relationship – an important factor in all forms of counselling or therapy. The psychodynamic model holds that the relationship between the client and his counsellor not only reflects the client's inner world but is also the most important vehicle in bringing about psychological change. This is because, although the client may experience us in a way that is concordant with his template for relationships, he has the opportunity not only to examine that template but also to learn what it is like to relate differently. Although other models do acknowledge the importance of the therapeutic relationship, no other model holds it as central in the process of bringing about change.

We are all resistant to change

When I first trained as a clinical psychologist using a cognitive behavioural model, I was puzzled by the fact that at times clients would ignore my suggestions about how they could bring about the change they so desperately longed for. Sometimes they would come back and tell me that they had not had time to do the assigned task that week, or that they had completely forgotten about it; sometimes they would say they had tried once and it didn't work so they gave up. They were not being deliberately difficult. Quite often they were upset at themselves that they were not doing the things they had agreed to. It was an example of how, even though in our conscious minds we want change, there is an unconscious resistance to doing so. There are many reasons for this, not least the fact that change is dangerous because it means stepping into the unknown. However painful our current predicament and however much we might want to be different, 'the devil you know' often feels preferable.

The psychodynamic model holds that resistance to change, and therefore to the process of counselling, is normal. Consequently, resistance is not seen as something that has to be got over before the client can start work; rather it is understood as a normal part of any therapeutic relationship. Psychodynamic models are interested in understanding what the resistance is about – in particular what the client finds difficult to give up in order to bring about the longed-for change. In our first meeting John gave me an indication about how difficult he might find it to change when he told me about what happened when he tried to talk to Anne about their relationship. When she had been angry, he had become ill; he needed to be looked after by her, and decided he would not risk upsetting her again. I hypothesized that he had dealt with his fear of change by retreating into illness and had regressed into a more dependent relationship with Anne. I needed to be aware that he might retreat from facing difficulty in his counselling with me, perhaps by becoming more dependent on Anne.

THREE

How Did We Get Here?

In the last chapter I talked about a number of agreed concepts currently in use in psychodynamic counselling. In this chapter I want to look at the route by which we arrived at these concepts. It is the story of the development of one of the defining ideas of the twentieth century, one that has become so embedded in our culture that its technical language has become part of everyday discourse – we are nearly all familiar with terms such as 'the unconscious', 'ego' or 'introversion/extroversion' for example. As well as explaining psychological distress, it has also contributed to our understanding of normal emotional development and psychological functioning. Furthermore, it has enriched our understanding of art, literature, religion, society and politics.

But it is also a human story of brilliance, friendship, rivalry, hatreds and politics. Freud had already made significant contributions to research in his first career as a neurologist in Vienna, when he turned his attention to psychological disturbance, in particular hysteria. Hysteria is rarely seen in Western society today, but was very common at the time. Sufferers experience physical symptoms, such as paralysis, for which there is no apparent physical cause. In 1893 Freud co-authored a landmark paper with his colleague Breuer in which they linked traumatic and unremembered events experienced in childhood with the physical symptoms of hysteria. Because the uncovered memories were about sexual trauma Freud later called his theory the Seduction Theory.

As patients could often only recall their memories of sexual trauma under hypnosis, Freud concluded that knowledge of the seduction was quite deliberately kept out of conscious memory because it was too painful. The concept of an unconscious mind was not, in itself, new but Freud was the first to propose the idea of the dynamic unconscious, and to understand it as the receptacle into which we deliberately banish or repress ideas or memories that we want to ignore. He argued that it is these repressed memories that cause neurotic illnesses. But why should we want to ignore them, how do we keep them out of consciousness and how do people recover from their neurotic illness once the ideas are conscious? Freud's attempts to answer these questions, and the techniques that he developed to help his patients access their memories, were the foundation of psychoanalysis.

Freud later downgraded the importance of actual trauma in childhood in favour of how well we deal with traumatic fantasies arising from our sexual instincts. Freud's theory, that from infancy a child's relationship with his parents is driven by the need to gratify his sexual instincts, was both revolutionary and controversial, and shocked many in the scientific community. He argued that our adult personality is the result of how we cope with our instinctual drives at different stages of development from infancy through to adolescence. He overturned theories of the mind by putting our inner world at the centre of mental life and early experience at the core of our adult personality.

Freud was a brilliant and creative thinker, who constantly revisited his theories in the light of new experience and understanding. But he was also a difficult man who did not brook dissent. Consequently, he fell out with most of his collaborators as they developed their ideas in ways he disapproved of. This included Jung, to whom he was close for many years, and whom he regarded as his heir. He was also a man of his time, whose theories were influenced by the dominant scientific culture of the nineteenth century, in particular Darwinism and physics. His ideas were also relentlessly phallo-centric. I spent much of my own psychodynamic training oscillating between admiration for his brilliance and anger at his downgrading of women's experience. Because Freud was such an exceptional thinker, and some of his ideas remain ego is conscious and part of it is unconscious. The ego is governed by the reality principle, meaning that its function is to stay in touch with the demands of the outside world. The need to repress unacceptable id urges is a great strain on the ego, and Freud hypothesized that the ego uses psychological defences to achieve some relief. At other times the ego's role is to find socially acceptable ways of meeting the id's needs. By doing this the ego begins to build skills and memories and emerges as a self. Psychodynamic practitioners often talk of 'ego strength', which is the capacity of a person to accept reality without having to use too many psychological defences to protect himself from it, while also not being under the undue influence of a harsh superego. Thinking of John, it was clear that a part of him wanted to go off to America and damn the consequences (an id wish), but his ego was in touch with the reality of the consequences should he do so.

Freud's theory of development

Freud's theory of development was extremely controversial because it was based on the effects of the sexual drive on various stages of the developing personality. Polite Viennese society found these ideas very difficult to accept, though, interestingly, they were less contentious than his original proposal that many children had, in fact, been sexually abused. Freud argued that children go through a series of psycho-sexual stages focused on different parts of the body, which he called 'erogenous zones'. The next stage of development could only be adequately negotiated following the successful resolution of the previous one. Freud argued that if a psycho-sexual stage is not adequately negotiated the child becomes stuck at that point in his development and his personality will become dominated by it.

The first is the oral stage, meaning that sexual pleasure is derived from the mouth through the enjoyment of sucking and biting. According to Freud the oral stage lasted until the child was one to one and a half years old and it culminated in weaning. He proposed that oral frustration led to personality characteristics such as envy and suspicion, while over-indulgence resulted in a tendency to idealize others. The second stage is the anal stage, when the child was approximately one to three years old. The erogenous zone is the anus and the focus is on the retention or expulsion of faeces and defecation is seen as the battle-ground for giving and withholding. Difficulties at this stage were hypothesized to lead to an anal expulsive character dominated by defiance and recklessness or an anal retentive character structure dominated by passive-aggression and withholding. The outcome of the anal stage was said to determine a person's attitudes towards authority and fair play.

In the phallic stage, when the child is approximately three to five years old, the erogenous zone is the genitals; this stage was the lynchpin of Freud's theory of personality. Freud proposed that at this stage the child unconsciously wished to possess the parent of the opposite gender and eliminate the same-sexed one. Known as the Oedipal complex, the idea is based on the Greek myth about Oedipus, who unknowingly married his mother after killing his father. According to Freud, all children wish to get rid of the same-sexed parent, who is seen as a rival for the possession of the opposite-sexed parent. However, there is a price to be paid for these wishes. The little boy becomes frightened that his father will punish him for wanting to possess his mother by castrating him, so he gives up his desire for his mother and identifies with his father. Freud argued that the superego develops out of the Oedipus complex in that through identification with the father the little boy internalizes his father's values and incorporates them into his developing superego. Failure to resolve the oedipal stage can lead to difficulties in intimate relationships, leading to jealousy and rivalry, and Freud hypothesized that it was the root of homosexuality.

In girls the presentation is slightly different and Freud proposed that they experience penis envy in response to realizing they do not have a penis. They blame their mother for not having one and fantasize wanting a child by their father, which in itself is a substitute for having a penis. He called this the electra conflict, and argued that girls resolve it by identifying with their mother to possess their father vicariously. Here Freud reveals the depth of his phallo-centrism as he never properly accounts for the experience in girls; instead he believed they could not fully resolve the oedipal conflict and did not have a properly functioning superego. They were therefore morally inferior to men.

Freud's theory was a 'one-person' theory, meaning that he considered that the most important determinant in a child's development was how he dealt with the strength of his own internal instincts. Relationships with the people around him were always much less important than reducing the tension arising from id instincts.

Current thinking

Few psychodynamic practitioners working today still use classical Freudian theory, though most use some of his concepts in a modified way. They have moved away from Freud's one-person psychology, and see the emerging self as being the product of the relationship between the baby and his carer/s. They no longer distinguish between the electra and Oedipus complex in the same way, though they still see the oedipal phase as developmentally important for both sexes. However, rather than understanding it as a drive, successful negotiation of the oedipal phase is understood as important in the development of the child's ability to cope with three-person relationships. Developmentally the child needs to cope with the fact that he does not have an exclusive relationship with either of his parents and that they have a relationship with each other that excludes him. At the same time he needs to realize that he is still loved and valued by them in order to feel of worth himself. If he can do this he can go on to cope with other relationships and successfully function as part of a group, where he needs to be aware that others have relationships that don't include him. Successful negotiation of the oedipal phase is also thought to contribute to our capacity to think in that we can step outside of our immediate experience (so that in a sense we take up the third position ourselves) and are able to reflect on that experience.

Carl Jung

Like Freud, Jung introduced concepts into our language that have entered common parlance. Amongst those are two of his most important contributions to psychodynamic thinking – that of introversion/extroversion and the concept of 'complex'. Other original concepts that are less well known are those of the collective unconscious, including archetypes, and the notion of synchronicity. Like Freud, Jung was also interested in dreams but, whereas Freud thought the manifest content of dreams disguised forbidden wishes, Jung saw dreams as being open and expressing something the dreamer does not know or understand. Whereas Freud thought dreams were difficult to comprehend because they were repressing something unwanted, Jung thought it was because they expressed themselves through symbols that needed to be understood. This difference nicely illustrates Jung's more optimistic view of the self compared with his one-time mentor. The other significant area of theory that Jung developed was to do with the development of the self.

Like Freud, Jung's was essentially a one-person psychology rather than a relational one. For example, he saw internal conflict as both inherent but also as necessary for growth and creativity. Jung, too, was a man of his time and in this part of his theory one can see the influence of nineteenth-century philosophers such as Hegel, who proposed that out of conflict came something new. Jung was also influenced by the ancient Greeks, both their philosophy (for example the theory of teleology, see below) and their mythology, which had a profound impact on his ideas.

Following his split from Freud, Jung named his approach 'analytical psychology', and this term is used today by Jungians, while Freudians use the term 'psychoanalytic' to describe their approach.

Jung's model of the psyche

Jung used the term 'psyche' rather than 'mind' because he understood it to encompass both conscious and unconscious functioning in a self-regulating system. He also believed that the psyche is teleological, meaning that it is innately purposeful, and that its purpose is to seek growth, wholeness and equilibrium. Jung called the search for wholeness the process of individuation, and involved becoming more conscious of oneself as a unique human being. Some would argue that Jung's ideas were a more positive way of understanding human development and nature than Freud's. To compare the two men's ideas is to face us not only with the content of those ideas, but also with the minds of their originators, and their own relationship to the world around them.

Jung proposed that the psyche strives to maintain the balance between opposing psychological qualities, for example the tendency to look inwards (introversion) or outwards (extroversion). He called introversion and extroversion the two 'attitudes'. Jung argued that introversion and extroversion are mutually exclusive, so could not exist consciously at the same time. However, if a person habitually favours one mode (for example, introversion), then, unconsciously, the other mode will act in a compensatory manner, which might then break through. This idea is similar to Freud's notion of the 'return of the repressed' when ideas actively pushed down into the unconscious by repression leak out unexpectedly.

Whether we are introverts or extroverts, we need to find a way to deal with the world, and Jung proposed that the psyche also has four 'functions', which are basic ways of doing so. 'Thinking' means evaluating ideas or information logically and involves decision-making or judgment. 'Feeling' is also about evaluating information, but through one's overall, emotional response to it. 'Sensation' is to do with getting information about the world through the senses, for example through looking and listening. Last is 'intuition', which is a form of perception that works outside the normal conscious process and comes from the complex integration of large amounts of information. While he considered thinking and feeling to be rational because they evaluate actual experience, Jung considered sensation and intuition to be irrational because they depend on an individual's perception. I think it is important to point out that Jung does not use the terms 'rational' and 'irrational' in the way we normally understand them, so he is not devaluing sensation and perception. Although we all have each of the four functions, according to Jung each of us has a superior function that is developed to a greater extent than the other three. We also have a secondary function, which we are aware of and is used to support the superior function. The tertiary function is slightly less developed than the other two, but is largely unconscious, while the inferior function is not only unconscious but also poorly developed. Jung believed it was important to develop and become conscious of all four functions.

The superior or dominant function not only operates in conjunction with the other functions but also in relation to our level of introversion and extroversion. By combining the two attitudes and the four functions Jung proposed the existence of eight psychological types, for example: extrovert thinking, introvert thinking, extrovert feeling, introverted feeling. Understanding her client's psychological type was felt to aid the counsellor's understanding of his world-view and value system and, as a result, perhaps his choice of vocation too. It may also help in understanding choice of romantic partner since people often choose someone who is strong in a function that is one of their less developed ones.

Like Freud, Jung understood the ego as standing at the junction of the inner and outer world. However, whereas Freud understood the ego as managing the competing demands of id and superego, Jung understood it more as an organizer of the four functions. He saw it as not only promoting survival but also as making life worth living. He argued that the ego develops from the self; again this stands in contrast to Freudian thinking which understands the self as emerging from the ego.

Jung also had a deep interest in what he called the 'shadow' part of our identity, the part of ourselves we do not wish to be. He felt that it is the hidden and repressed part of ourselves; it is the repository of the part of us that is unwanted and disowned and which is seen as being the uncivilized, inferior and animal part of us. It is also seen as potential that has not been realized; Jung argued that unless these were recognized and owned we would be deprived of connectedness with other people and sources of energy to live life to the full. He consequently saw counselling as an opportunity to make the shadow conscious in order to become more rounded and whole.

The collective unconscious

The idea of the collective unconscious is central to Jung's theory and a major departure from Freud's. Like Freud, Jung subscribed to the idea of a conscious mind as well as what he called the personal unconscious; these are respectively the first and second layers of the mind. Like Freud, Jung understood that the personal unconscious contained repressed material, which was unacceptable to the conscious mind. However, he also held the view that there was a further, 'third', layer beyond the conscious and personal unconscious, which was biologically based and shared by all humankind. This he called the 'collective unconscious'. He believed that all human beings share an inherited part of the unconscious mind which organizes and structures experience in a similar way, and that consequently some functioning is inherited. He proposed that the personal unconscious comes out of the interaction between the collective unconscious and the development of the individual across the life-span and consists of a personal reservoir of experiences that are unique to each individual and not necessarily organized in the same way in each person.

Jung accounted for the idea of a collective unconscious through his theory of archetypes. Archetypes predispose people to experience life in a particular way and are expressed through archetypal images that are common to all cultures, for example the wise old man and the hero appear in the narratives of all cultures. Archetypes themselves are unconscious, so they cannot be directly observed; they have to be inferred through images, symbols and patterns of behavior which are conscious. Archetypes can also be deduced by examining images, art and myths across cultures. Jung proposed that the shadow can also be an archetype, and is found in the existence of evil.

Jung's theory of synchronicity is based on the idea that simultaneous occurrences can be meaningfully related to one another, without having an underlying causal relationship. In other words, things don't happen just by chance but neither are they caused. Jung regarded such events as 'meaningful coincidence'. He argued that synchronistic events can reveal an underlying pattern or conceptual framework which underlies the whole of human experience and history. It was for this reason he saw synchronicity as conclusive evidence for the existence of a collective unconscious and the associated archetypes.

Complexes

Although Freud used the term 'complex' in relation to the Oedipal and electra complexes, it was Jung who really elaborated the concept. Jung understood the complex as a collection of mental factors, such as images and ideas, which are connected unconsciously. Jung described a complex as being a 'node' in the unconscious, which is autonomous and behaves as though it is independent of the person. By their nature, complexes are not conscious, but instead can be detected through a person's behaviour, since they influence both attitudes and behaviour. One of the most commonly referred to complexes is an 'inferiority' complex, in which a cluster of negative beliefs and behaviours about the self become manifest in the way the person acts and how he relates to himself, for example by putting himself down or always behaving as though his needs do not matter. People observing complexes are often puzzled by them, for example when someone is very good at something but always puts down his achievements. Other times observers can be irritated, for example when someone displays a 'superiority' complex in which they act as though they and their ideas are more important than others.

Current thinking

At one time people who chose Jungian counselling tended to be those whose focus was more towards an integration of their adult selves or their spiritual lives rather than working through the developmental roots of their difficulties. In part this was because Jung himself did not describe a coherent developmental theory, instead arguing that the self did not become manifest until middle life. It fell to Michael Fordham, who was trained as a Jungian analyst, but who also worked with children, to work out a model of development for analytical psychology. From his observations of young children, Fordham concluded that the self was present in infancy and he introduced the idea of a primary self to account for his view that the infant is an individual, though yet immature, self which develops out of contact with the environment.

He saw the primary self as the potential for who the infant might become. He also proposed that there were two, twin, processes involved in the development of the self – that of deintegration and reintegration. Fordham moved analytical psychology away from the heavy emphasis on the metaphysical, which had been so controversial but central to Jung's thinking, towards a theory more grounded in developmental psychology.

Early in his career Fordham was a contemporary of Klein, and some of his thinking incorporates ideas that can be traced to her; he was also influenced by Bion and, later, Winnicott. Fordham has been described as positioning contemporary analytical psychology between modern psychoanalysis and Jung's original formulations. Certainly contemporary Jungian and psychoanalytic approaches have much in common in terms of the theory and practice of counselling, though sometimes they are divided by the language they use. Modern Jungians, like modern Freudians, use Jung's original ideas as a platform that informs their thinking rather than a straitjacket that constrains them. Thus, the following sections on Klein, Winnicott, Bowlby and neuroscience have as many implications for the development of current analytical psychology approaches as they do for psychoanalytic thinking.

A number of Jung's original ideas have found modern expression, in the way that Freud's have. For example, his notion of the teleological, or purposeful, nature of the mind can be found in modern therapies like Mentalization-Based Treatment. And his idea that there is a common, inherited, neurological basis for some of our behaviour and preconceptions is also reflected in modern theory about the neurological basis for behaviour.

Melanie Klein

Early in her career as a child analyst, Klein had noticed that she was observing processes in pre-oedipal children that were similar to the oedipal conflicts of older children. She therefore concluded that the superego was in operation long before the age assigned it by Freud and felt it belonged to the oral phase. This led her to a radical rethink of Freud's developmental theory and ultimately theories of how adult minds work too.

Freud's theory had emerged largely from his work with adults. Inevitably the information we gain about childhood by listening to adults is unlikely to be an accurate account of childhood experience. Klein worked with children and her theories were influenced by direct observation. She was also in a position where she could develop her theories away from Freud's watchful eye, as she moved to London in the 1920s. Taken as a whole, however, although Klein's work transformed some of Freud's ideas, it was also an extension of his theory.

One effect was to bring forward the point at which mental illness developed – Klein dated it during the first year of life, whereas Freud dated it at the oedipal stage at around three to five years. For Klein the baby entered the world and began to relate to people straight away, implying a significant level of cognitive complexity. Klein argued that it was the internalization of these early object relationships that determined the child's inner world. One of the implications of this was that mothers became very important, since they were the carers of very small babies, whereas in classical Freudian theory fathers were seen to have the crucial impact on personality development. This change in emphasis has had significant ramifications, to the extent that fathers' contribution to child development became a relatively neglected subject in the second half of the twentieth century, which has only recently begun to be rectified.

Klein developed Freud's idea of the death instinct, which he had conceptualized to account for the destruction of the First World War, and gave it a central place in her theory. An important part of Klein's death instinct was the notion of innate envy, which she saw as being a particularly malignant form of the death instinct since it sought to destroy that which is good. She felt that envy was particularly destructive to relationships because its attack was not on a bad object, but on the good object. Klein's proposal that envy is innate, rather than the result of inadequate parenting and a frustrating environment, was one of the major points of disagreement, not only with Freudians, but with the later Object Relations theorists in the Independent School.

Klein and fantasy

Klein proposed that unconscious fantasy was central to mental life from the moment of birth. She saw it as an instinctual capacity, and proposed that a baby's fantasies determined how he experienced the outer world and ultimately how, as an adult, he experienced the world around him. She placed such an emphasis on unconscious fantasy that she has been criticized for ignoring what was going on in the real world and the baby's experience of the real mother. However, she drew our attention to the fact that our fantasies about relationships do not always reflect the actual relationship; fantasy can both interpret and distort events. As a consequence, inner object relationships may be different from the actual relationship with a parent and may be more problematic than external ones. Many counsellors will attest to the fact that as a client becomes less disturbed his parents turn from being ogres into being merely human. This is because he has less of a need to project into them his powerful and destructive fantasies.

One of Klein's most controversial proposals was that babies are born with a built-in knowledge of parental sexual intercourse, with a rudimentary sense of a vagina and a penis. This is the point where many part company with Klein, partly because her language is so uncompromising and concrete. But taken at a more symbolic level, she was pointing to a complexity of cognitive functioning in small babies that Freud had not imagined. Although many would disagree with her ideas regarding an actual notion of parental intercourse, the notion of early cognitive complexity is in keeping with the findings of modern research into babies' development.

Klein's theory of development

Klein proposed two important stages in development: the paranoid-schizoid position and the depressive position. The paranoid-schizoid position is present at birth and dominates for the first six months. She argued that the very small baby does not relate to his objects as whole people, but rather experiences each aspect of his mother separately – what

Klein called part-objects. So he experiences her eyes, her nipple, and her hair as separate from one another. For Klein the most important part-object is the breast. When the baby is hungry he fantasizes the breast as something bad through the process of projecting his discomfort of hunger into it. In turn he feels he is being attacked back (persecuted) by the bad breast. The notion of persecution highlights the central position that Klein gives to destructive and aggressive feelings. For her, babies live in a world in which envy, hatred and aggression are just as important, or even more so, than love. When the baby is being fed the breast is experienced not only as good but as something completely different from the bad breast. This notion of things being wholly good or wholly bad led Klein to conceptualize early development as being dominated by the experience of the world being an extreme place in which good and bad can change places very quickly. In order to deal with these feelings of persecutory anxiety Klein proposes that the baby develops defence mechanisms from birth.

The depressive position should not be confused with depression. Klein's notion of a position is a description of how we position ourselves in relation to an object. The depressive position involves the recognition of sadness and loss, but does not mean the person *is* depressed. The depressive position is something we achieve and not everyone achieves it as their dominant mode of functioning. It has the potential to develop at about six months, but can only be reached once we have achieved an ability to experience the good and bad breast as belonging to the same person. This involves important changes in mental functioning, including beginning to think of people as whole objects and recognizing mother as a separate person. Unless we can achieve the depressive position we cannot relate to our objects in a mature way, because we do not perceive them as separate from us with their own feelings and needs.

Klein named it the depressive position because it involves the baby feeling guilty because of the damage he believes he has caused his mother through his fantasized attacks on her. This is followed by an attempt to repair the object the baby has damaged. In order to achieve, or work through, the depressive position the child has to learn that however angry he is, he is still loved. However, he also has to learn to take responsibility for his own aggression and not project it into other people. In achieving the depressive position we are able to develop a capacity for concern about our objects – we begin to imagine what it might be like to be them. In some ways we have to constantly work to hold on to the depressive position as adults, as paranoid anxieties are always threatening to break through.

Klein believed that normal psychological functioning involves moving between the paranoid-schizoid and the depressive positions. However, the more we relate to other people in a paranoid-schizoid way, the more disturbed our object relationships and our internal world will be. However, there are situations where paranoid-schizoid functioning becomes more dominant in the normal course of events. One of these is in groups, where we tend to experience a heightened sense of persecutory anxiety. This is probably because it is difficult to get the feedback from a group of people that we are safe and will not be attacked. In this sense the paranoid-schizoid position might be considered adaptive since it keeps us alert to possible danger in a situation where it is difficult to know what's going on in everyone's mind.

The Oedipus complex

Klein agreed with Freud that the Oedipus complex was important in terms of psychological development, but disagreed with him about its timing. She located the Oedipus complex in the first year of life, and with it the pain of recognizing that the baby is excluded from the relationship between his parents. In order to successfully resolve the conflict he has to bring the two (one loved, the other hated) together in his mind, which is part of the depressive position.

Current thinking

Although her theory was more concerned with relationships than Freud's, Klein's theory was not fully a two-person psychology. By emphasizing the role of fantasy to the extent she did, she did not fully recognize the importance of the actual mother in the development of her child. Later Kleinian theorists have taken the role of real experience more seriously, and acknowledged that environmental failure or trauma affect the way in which fantasy develops, recognizing that there is a much more complex interaction between the two than Klein originally thought.

Another major development in modern Kleinian thinking is the concept of 'containment', first proposed by one of the major post-Kleinians, Bion. He proposed that babies project their raw fantasies and feelings into their mother and that she accepts them and transforms them into something less frightening before giving them back. It is rather like the process by which parent birds partially digest food before giving it to their chicks, so that the chicks can themselves more easily digest it. If it is not partially digested the chick cannot cope with what is being fed to him. In the same way in the therapeutic relationship the counsellor takes the raw projections of her client and, by containing and transforming them, gives them back to him in a way that is not so threatening.

Donald Winnicott

Winnicott was a paediatrician and a psychoanalyst. Along with Michael Balint and Ronald Fairbairn, he was one of the most influential thinkers in the Object Relations School. His vast experience with children (over 20,000 consultations with mothers and their children) led him to develop innovative ideas about child development, which he then translated into his analytic work with children and adults. Winnicott did not produce a coherent theory of his own and had no wish to found a school; he was a truly Independent thinker. Rather, he developed a series of linked ideas about the relationship between babies and their carers which were very original, and which have created a number of concepts that are now current in our everyday language, for example 'good enough' parenting and 'transitional object'. Like Klein, he gave mothers a central place in infant development, away from Freud's emphasis on the father.

Winnicott disagreed with Freud that our prime need is to seek pleasure, instead placing the primary focus on our needs for intimacy and connection with other people. He disagreed with Klein about the importance of fantasy in development, particularly the death instinct. However, he did not dismiss the role of fantasy entirely. Rather, he conceptualized children's development as the result of a real relationship with a real parent, with fantasies being developed in the context of that relationship. Unlike Klein, therefore, he saw envy and other manifestations of aggression as the result of failures in the environment rather than caused by an innate predisposition in the child.

Winnicott argued that a baby cannot exist psychologically without a mother who mirrors his experience and adapts to him; in this sense he was proposing a true two-person psychology. Winnicott proposed that in the third trimester of pregnancy a mother enters a particular state of mind, 'primary maternal preoccupation', in which she becomes increasingly identified with and absorbed by her baby. This state of mind continues into the first few months of the baby's life and enables the mother to be particularly sensitive to her baby's needs. Through this sensitivity the mother allows her baby to have the illusion of being in charge of the relationship. So, for example, if the mother quickly responds to her baby's cry and picks him up he can imagine that he has created her. This level of omnipotence was considered by Winnicott as vital in the early months.

If his mother does not respond when the baby cries, he might fall into an 'unbearable state of anxiety' where he feels completely alone. If, on the other hand, she responds when he does not need her he will feel that she has intruded inappropriately, or 'impinged on' him, in Winnicott's terminology. Winnicott felt that the baby's emerging ego was vulnerable to being overwhelmed by impingements from the environment and that it was the mother who could protect him from the extremes of psychological discomfort and distress. By providing what Winnicott called a 'holding environment' the mother enabled the baby to naturally become autonomous.

Some mothers are unable to prevent impingements and the baby will protect himself from this failure in her sensitivity by becoming prematurely autonomous and developing a false self. The false self is compliant (not protesting, for example, if he is picked up when he doesn't want to be) and exists to protect the baby's true self from the hurt of the failure in the relationship with his mother. In later life such a baby would grow up to have difficulties in forming truly intimate relationships, since his false self cannot allow him to be truly close to another person. Instead he might have relationships that are superficial but which are ultimately unsatisfactory and leave him feeling lonely.

Winnicott did not demand that mothering must be absolutely perfect. Rather he said it needed to be 'good enough'. By that he meant that the baby can tolerate some failure in sensitivity, as long as it is not too much. The amount of frustration a baby can tolerate will increase as he becomes older and his ego becomes stronger. Maternal sensitivity at this stage is about knowing how much frustration a baby can comfortably manage before he is overwhelmed.

The other truly innovative idea that Winnicott introduced was that of the transitional object. Most of you will be familiar with how important a comforter (usually a toy or a corner of a blanket) can be for a toddler. He can tolerate being away from his mother so long as he has his comforter, or transitional object. The important thing about a transitional object is that the baby must choose it himself. This is because it is a representation of his mother, and therefore can only be created by him. Winnicott called it a *transitional* object because it represented both the mother and something separate from her. It facilitates a transition from the stage of absolute dependency on the mother to the beginning of psychologically separating and becoming more autonomous.

Winnicott's greatest contribution stems from his innovations in therapeutic technique. He created a holding environment which allowed his patients to regress to a level of dependency where he was able recreate important aspects of the early relationship with their mother. The re-working of this early relationship through transference is seen by modern Object Relations theorists as being the most important element in therapy. The function of the therapist as a real person is important too and later theorists have argued that one of the most influential factors leading to change in therapy is the discovery of the counsellor as a new object with whom the client can develop a real relationship.

John Bowlby and attachment theory

Although Bowlby was a psychoanalyst, he had always had misgivings about the scientific status of psychoanalysis. His original hope had been to scientifically underpin psychoanalysis, but he fell out with the psychoanalytic establishment and as a result his contributions were largely ignored for two decades.

During the Second World War Bowlby had become involved in researching delinquent children and concluded that actual separation from parents was both damaging and a factor in delinquency. This research led to an interest in the consequences of maternal deprivation, and, combined with an interest in ethology,[1] he began to write about the importance of sensitive periods in a baby's attachment to his mother,[2] and the negative effects of early separation. As a result he made, what were then, controversial suggestions about the importance of actual experience which he felt was much more significant in development than fantasy. In particular, he proposed that psychological problems are the result of deficiencies in a child's psychological environment rather than instinctual conflict. Unlike Winnicott, who was proposing similar ideas but still using many of the theories and conventions of psychoanalysis, Bowlby was more uncompromising in his dissent from the dominant thinking of the time, which was still heavily influenced by Klein.

Attachment research proliferated in the field of child development in the 1970s and 1980s and I will refer to 'attachment theory' when not specifically identifying Bowlby's contributions. During this time of proliferation Bowlby's work, and that of others in the field such as Ainsworth and Main, went largely unnoticed in the psychodynamic world. However, there was a resurgence of interest in his ideas in the

1990s. This rekindling of interest is partly the result of the work of psychoanalytically-oriented developmental researchers like Daniel Stern, who brought the findings in infant research to the attention of the psychodynamic world. It is also attributable to the work of researchers at the Anna Freud Centre in London, including Peter Fonagy. Fonagy has been one of the main proponents in creating a rapprochement between modern psychoanalytic thinking and attachment research, and this has resulted in new dynamic approaches including Mentalization-Based Therapy, which is specifically oriented to the needs of borderline clients. Also, we now live in a world of evidence-based practice and psychodynamic theories have been under attack because of their difficulty in substantiating their claims of therapeutic change in the paradigm that is currently regarded as the best way of evaluating therapies. Attachment theory has been seen as holding the promise of a scientific validation of some of those theories.

Bowlby's model has been called 'bio-psycho-social' meaning that it recognizes the importance of a biological drive to create social relationships, which creates our psychological selves. As a species we have developed social groupings that rely on co-operation and understanding between individuals to maximize our chances of survival. To do this there need to be strong bonds between individuals to maintain the functioning of the group. Bowlby suggested that babies developed a strong bond to their mothers as a result of an in-built biological drive. He conceptualized this in Darwinian terms and argued that in a hostile world the baby who is securely attached to and stays close to his mother maximizes his chances of surviving into adulthood. Observable attachment behaviour such as crying on separation and searching is at its maximum between 12 and 18 months, which is the age at which babies would be at risk from accidentally straying from their mothers as they become independently mobile.

Bowlby proposed that the mother becomes a 'secure base' from which the baby can explore the world around him. When mother is present the baby is able to explore, but when she is not he becomes focused on finding her again and cannot explore until he does so. The secure base is initially the actual person of the mother, but, Bowlby argued, the attachment relationship between baby and mother becomes internalized and the secure base becomes a mental representation of that relationship. A relationship that is sensitive towards the child's needs creates a child who can be aware of others' needs, which moderates levels of aggression and facilitates group functioning. Bowlby called the way we represent our relationships an internal working model. It is our internal working model that holds in it the template of our relationships to our carers and is later transferred to other relationships (for example a counsellor). It determines how we see ourselves through their eyes and how we see them. Now, this is not dissimilar to other Object Relations theories, but Bowlby went so far in downgrading the role of fantasy and imagination that other psychodynamic thinkers feel that he has not sufficiently allowed for the distortions that occur as a result of how we construct what happens to us.

Attachment theory proposes, and infant research has confirmed that, from the moment of birth, babies are programmed to relate to their caregivers, and that it is the quality of that interaction that will profoundly influence a child's later development. In common with Winnicott, attachment theory argues that maternal sensitivity is the key to the quality of a baby's attachment to his mother. Put simply, mothers who are sensitive to their baby's needs will rear securely attached babies and children. Those who lack sensitivity to their baby's needs will rear children who are insecurely attached; an example is a mother who regularly ignores her baby's cries then picks him up when she wants to play rather than when the baby is ready to. This does not mean the baby will have no attachment to his mother, but rather that he will develop an internal working model of a mother who does not respond to his needs and a self who is not worthy of being responded to. As a result he may become anxiously attached, meaning that he cannot either be soothed by his mother or explore away from her. Such babies are often described as 'clingy'. Alternatively he may become avoidantly attached, meaning that he would try to pretend his mother is not important and he doesn't need her.

In the first three years of life babies develop different attachments to different important people in their lives, so they can be securely attached to one parent and insecurely attached to the other. But by the time he is three the baby will have internalized the most influential of his attachment relationships and that is the one that will dominate. There is evidence that childhood attachment patterns continue into adulthood, and that they are passed on to the next generation. However, attachment is not necessarily fixed for life at this point, and there is evidence that a child's attachment status can change in response to a change in his circumstances. Previously securely attached children can become insecurely attached as the result of sexual abuse, for example. Alternatively, an insecurely attached child might become securely attached if, say, a depressed mother becomes well again and able to be in tune with her child. Attachment status can also change as the result of therapy, and research has shown that insecurely attached adults can become more securely attached following therapeutic interventions. One of the main advantages of being securely attached is that it facilitates mental health. Securely attached adults are more able to make intimate relationships, which itself is a protection against psychological distress.

Bowlby argued that attachment feelings – the need to be close to someone we feel will protect and care for us – can be activated at any time in our lives. He therefore conceptualized losing someone, say the death of a partner in later life, as an attachment crisis because we become separated from a loved one. People who have been bereaved often show some of the behaviours that we observe in small children separated from their parents, such as searching. Starting counselling can also be understood as an attachment crisis, when our need to be cared for by someone stronger than ourselves is heightened by whatever distress has taken us there.

Developments in psychodynamic thinking

Recent contributors to psychodynamic theory

I have concentrated in this chapter on some of the major psychodynamic theorists who have revolutionized our thinking. But I would like to finish by acknowledging a few of the more recent thinkers who are currently developing our understanding, or who have done so in the recent past. Joseph Sandler, and his wife Anne-Marie, are two of the most influential modern Contemporary Freudians, and their particular contribution was to situate Freud's drive theory within a two-person psychology; Peter Fonagy is also a Contemporary Freudian. After Fordham, some of the most influential Jungians are Andrew Samuels, Jean Knox and Hester Solomon, who have further developed Fordham's theoretical thrust. Modern Kleinian thinkers include Hannah Segal, Elizabeth Bott Spillius, Edna O'Shaughnessy, Herbert Rosenberg, Otto Kernberg and Ronald Britton. Together these writers have not only brought Klein's theory up to date, but have made her ideas, which at times can be experienced as uncompromising, more accessible. Modern Independent thinkers include Juliet Mitchell, Nina Coltart, Christopher Bollas, Phil Mollon and Neville Symington. The Independents have also been active in making links with members of the American Relational School, for example Jessica Benjamin, and the Self-Psychologists for example, Heinz Kohut. Peter Fonagy and Jeremy Holmes have both integrated and advanced our understanding of attachment theory and psychodynamic approaches.

Psychodynamic theory and neuroscience

The beginning of the twenty-first century is an exciting time to come into psychodynamic counselling, and in examining the role of modern neuroscience in psychodynamic thinking we return to the origins of our discipline, since Freud's first career was as a neurologist. In the last 20 years there has been an explosion in our understanding of how our brain develops and functions, which has brought neuroscience and developmental theory together, underscoring the value of the psychodynamic approach to psychological difficulties. In particular there is an increasing understanding of the role of early experience in how the brain is sculpted, so that we can no longer think about nature (what we are born with) and nurture (the influence of our experience) as rivals in how we understand development, as has traditionally been the case. Instead we are beginning to unravel the complex relationship between the two, and how they impact on one-another. For example, it has been discovered that the structure of our brains is formed by the experience we have as very young babies. This occurs because, although we are born with all the brain cells we will ever have, the connections between those brain cells happen as the result of the relationship between the baby and his carers (this is what we mean by 'early experience'). The cells that don't become connected die off, while those that do make ever richer connections, which then determine how the baby experiences the world. Writers such as Alan Schore, who is a neuropsychologist as well as a psychotherapist, have brought together the findings of neuroscience and psychotherapy to account for both development and change in emotional processing.

Brain scans from children brought up in Romanian orphanages during the Communist period show little connectiveness in the social brain – the areas of the brain associated with relationships. These children were often left alone for most of the day and experienced little or no sensitive interaction with caregivers. By comparison, babies who have the opportunity to relate to their carers have much higher levels of connectiveness in their social brains. Children from the orphanages in Romania have been found to have little capacity to relate to other people; in particular they have little capacity for empathy, and it is hypothesized that it is the lack of connectivity in their social brains that causes this. This has enormous impact on their adult behaviour. For example, the Romanian secret police, the Stasi, who were known for their brutality, recruited many of their members from orphanages. This was because those reared in them were known to lack empathy and were therefore ideally suited to the kinds of practices common in the Stasi.

The brain is at its most plastic (that is, can generate new connections between cells) during childhood, but new learning, including emotional learning, can take place in adulthood so long as the right conditions apply. This explains both why people can change in adulthood, and also why some kinds of early experience are difficult to repair, but instead need to be managed (for example through Cognitive

Behavioural Therapy). Several authors have suggested that a number of features of dynamic work may be particularly implicated in facilitating the growth of new connections in the brain:

- The optimal conditions for creating new connections in the brain are created by a combination of emotional arousal and cognitive understanding. Psychodynamic approaches are well-placed to safely create the 'safe emergency' that leads to the kind of emotional arousal that is most likely to lead to change.
- The setting in psychodynamic work is established to maximize the potential for the kind of safe and empathic relationship which allows for the safe expression of difficult feelings – the safe emergency.
- The importance that psychodynamic practitioners place on seeing the world through their clients' eyes recreates the early experience of being accurately mirrored by an important other, which is so essential to the development of the self. This is facilitated by interpretation.
- The co-construction of autobiographical narrative facilitates the development of a sense of self and one's place in one's own history, which helps in the process of integration.
- The psychodynamic model is the only 'mainstream' therapeutic model that values regression as a way of re-creating the emotional environment necessary to enable the client to work through past hurts and developmental deficits in the consulting room.

It is possible that, in the future, we may be able to show the difference between brain activity before and after a given therapeutic intervention. This is not only good news in terms of evidence-based practice, but it means we may soon have the opportunity to find out which of our techniques works with whom; at present a very hit and miss affair in all forms of counselling.

Authors like Mark Solms, who is both a psychoanalyst and a neuroscientist, have written about how we can relate some of the concepts of psychodynamic thinking to the information coming out of neuroscience. For example, the lack of empathy seen in Romanian orphans is similar to the lack of the capacity for concern described by Klein in those people who do not achieve the depressive position. Solms has suggested ways in which concepts such as libido might also begin to map onto brain anatomy and chemistry. However, as Solms counsels, we are still at the very early stages of being able to track these concepts, and there is a distance to go before we will be able to answer such questions as 'is there really such a thing as repression?' What is clear is that the continuing dialogue between psychodynamics and neuroscience holds the promise of an exciting future for both.

Notes

1 The science of species-specific biologically-driven (instinctual) behaviour.
2 For the sake of simplicity I will continue to refer to the primary carer as 'mother'; however, I acknowledge that primary carers can also be fathers, grandparents and so on.

FOUR

Putting Concepts into Practice: What Happens in Psychodynamic Counselling?

Earlier in the book I proposed that the therapeutic model we adhere to is a determining factor in the way we, as practitioners, both relate to our clients and conduct counselling sessions. There is in addition the question of personal style, which also plays a part in how we behave in the consulting room. Psychodynamic counsellors, no less than anyone else, are likely to choose a theoretical position that chimes with, and maybe even justifies, their personal style and beliefs. Furthermore, although psychodynamic counsellors are guided by broadly similar concepts, the interpretation of those concepts leads to a variation in practice. So, bearing in mind personal differences and the variation across the different approaches within the psychodynamic model, what is a typical first session like for a client?

The first session

The first thing a new client will notice is that a psychodynamic counsellor is likely to be quite formal in the way she relates to him, both when setting up the appointment and when greeting him; she may use surnames rather than first names, for example. She will also be unlikely to engage in social conversation on the way to and from the consulting room or during the session. The client will probably notice that the consulting room is not particularly personalized, even if it is in the counsellor's own home: there won't be family photos on display, for example. During the session the counsellor is unlikely to undertake a formal predetermined assessment and ask a lot of questions, rather she is likely to listen to the client's story and prompt as necessary. The atmosphere in the consulting room is usually quite calm and unhurried. The counsellor will listen very carefully to what the client says, and is unlikely to make notes during the session. She will probably be fairly unobtrusive in the way she relates to her client, although this will not be in a cold way. The comments she makes may be to seek clarification, ask a question, make links between aspects of the client's story or offer an interpretation about what the client has said. Sometimes that interpretation will refer to the client's thoughts about the counsellor.

If asked personal questions, for example 'have you got any children?', she will seek to find out why the question is important, rather than immediately answering it, and indeed will be unlikely to disclose that kind of personal information at all. The client will notice that the counsellor does not offer advice or come up with solutions to problems, but rather helps him to take note of what he himself is saying or feeling. Her comments on the whole will make him more aware of what he thinks and feels and how he acts, and will help him to explore rather than problem-solve. The client should feel that he has been listened to carefully and that his feelings are taken seriously. At the end of the session the counsellor will not set him any tasks to be completed by the next session, which can be a surprise for those who have had previous counselling in other approaches where between-session assignments have been set.

All of the above ways of relating to the client are theory-driven and are intended to facilitate a safe environment in which the client can talk about his problems and begin to explore his inner world. In the sections below I will look at this in more detail.

The establishment of a holding environment

The reason for much of what I have described above is that psychodynamic practitioners pay especial attention to issues such as the setting in which counselling takes place and the boundaries around counselling. This is in order to facilitate an environment that feels safe and predictable so that the client has a space in which he is free to explore those areas of his life that are painful. This may elicit childhood as well as adult hurts and fantasies. The creation of a safe space enables the client to feel held by the treatment, which is itself a significant therapeutic factor.

Ideally counselling takes place in a setting that minimally impinges on the client, so that he is free from unnecessary distractions and is more able to be in touch with his inner world. Wherever possible the client is seen in the same room at the same time on the same day of the week. This facilitates a sense of rhythm and security about his counselling, which will anchor him when he is working with areas of uncertainty later. It can be difficult for a client to have a sense of an ongoing relationship with his counsellor and experience her as someone who is trustworthy if she is constantly changing his session times or the room in which she sees him.

The reason psychodynamic counsellors avoid over-personalizing their room is in order to protect the client from being overwhelmed by personal information he might find difficult to cope with. Some psychodynamic practitioners have no items of personal significance in their consulting rooms. They argue that if they give too much away about themselves it will inhibit the client's capacity to fantasize or will impose their personality on the client. More usually, counsellors personalize their rooms in a limited way, by hanging pictures or having flowers or ornaments. They argue that we already give away quite a bit about ourselves through the clothes or jewellery we wear, our body language or our choice of furniture in a consulting room. Furthermore, they argue that counselling takes place through the medium of a relationship and that the person of the counsellor needs to be real as well as neutral.

Part of the holding environment involves the client having an experience of the counsellor giving him her undivided attention. So it is important that the setting should be private and free from interruption. It is difficult for clients to allow themselves to be vulnerable and build up trust in the counsellor if they are always concerned that should someone knock at the door the counsellor will answer it, or that she might attend to a telephone ringing in the room. It can be much more difficult to control privacy and interruptions in the public sector than when working in private practice. It is also easier for the counsellor to provide a holding or containing environment for her client if she herself feels comfortable and safe in her physical environment. This is a further reason for having a room that is used regularly by the counsellor and is dedicated to therapy.

Boundaries are particularly important in psychodynamic work and contribute to the feeling of being contained by the counsellor. Many of these boundaries are common to all counselling approaches, such as confidentiality and not entering into a social or sexual relationship with the client. Other boundaries are more closely observed by psychodynamic practitioners than those from other orientations. The most immediately obvious boundary is that of time. The normal length of a session is 50 minutes, and practitioners are usually punctual about starting and finishing on time. This enables the client to know how long his session will be, when he can expect it to end and that he has a specific time in which to work. It also contributes to a feeling of safety as the client can infer that if the counsellor is punctilious about one type of boundary (for example, time) then she will be punctilious about other types of boundary (for example, confidentiality). Not surprisingly, the client can sometimes also find time boundaries difficult, particularly if he has arrived late or he gets to something very painful just as the session is ending. But we might wonder why a client is late, or says the most painful or important things just as the session is about to finish.

> Charlotte frequently arrived late for her session, and was then frustrated when the session ended before she was ready. When her counsellor, Mike, tried to help her think about why she was late so often she said she couldn't help it, as the traffic was unpredictable at that time of day. She was his last client of the day and Mike wondered if he should offer to change her session time to give her more time to get to him. Discussing this with his supervisor, he remembered that as a child Charlotte had arrived home from school some time before her mother had returned from work. She would sit and wait for her, alone in the

house, never knowing when her mother would arrive home. Mike and his supervisor realized that, in keeping him waiting, Charlotte might be communicating to him, through the countertransference, what it was like to not know when someone was going to arrive. He therefore decided to explore this with her before offering to change her session time.

Therapeutic neutrality

The counsellor's neutrality and the atmosphere she therefore creates in her consulting room is one of the distinguishing features of psychodynamic work. The atmosphere in a psychodynamic practitioner's room should facilitate thoughtfulness, becoming aware of one's own internal processes and feeling free to express emotion. Earlier I described how the counsellor would be quite formal, and would not engage in social conversation or give personal information away. To do this often involves the counsellor behaving in a way that subsumes her normal personality or personal style. She has to hold back from responding in ways that she might normally do, for example not offering reassurance or advice to a client who is distressed. This is called therapeutic abstinence as it involves abstaining from projecting one's own personality too much into the therapeutic space.

Clients can initially experience neutrality as coldness or lack of caring, though as the work progresses they often come to value it and recognize the value of being protected from the counsellor imposing her needs or beliefs. Therapeutic neutrality should facilitate the client in exploring his own responses and solutions and deepen the transference, including the negative transference, by which I mean feelings of anger or disappointment with the counsellor. Many clients come to counselling having difficulties with the experience or expression of negative feelings, and one of the tasks of psychodynamic work is to help them to do so. This can be hard to do as, like most of us, counsellors usually have a need to be liked. One of the reasons new counsellors can find therapeutic abstinence hard to practise is that they are aware that their holding back may well produce negative feelings in the client. Neutrality can therefore be quite a strain for both counsellor and client.

When Freud first wrote about the transference his ideal was that the analyst should engage in neutrality in order to become a 'blank screen' onto which the client could project his inner world. He argued that by revealing nothing of herself she enabled the client to play out his transference to her on an empty stage. Indeed, the caricature of the psychodynamic practitioner involves a silent counsellor or therapist who engages very little with her client. Today we view the blank screen as both impossible and undesirable. Modern psychodynamic practitioners understand that being completely abstinent is not just being neutral, but might actually re-traumatize a client who has been brought up by parents who were distant or withholding. In Freud's day it was believed that revealing and working through the transference was sufficient to bring about change. We now recognize that between them, client and counsellor develop a real and unique relationship in which the counsellor becomes a 'new object' for the client, and not just a transference object. To do this requires a real and spontaneous relationship between client and counsellor, while still involving sufficient neutrality to facilitate the transference and to prevent impingement of the counsellor on the client.

Clients can find therapeutic abstinence very difficult since they will probably never have had another relationship as an adult that is so one-sided. The amount a psychodynamic counsellor reveals of herself varies according to theoretical orientation and, I think, individual preference as well. My personal stance is that what I reveal will be determined by whether telling my client something about me would progress or hinder the work we are doing. I also need to feel personally happy about what I reveal. If I do reveal personal information I believe it is important for clients to explore their fantasies about the matter in hand first. Having done that it can then be important to explore reality and how that fits with the fantasy.

After I had been seeing John for about nine months I took an extended break over Christmas because I had a teaching commitment that took me abroad. John became quite convinced that I was ill and going into hospital for an operation. In exploring this fantasy with him we began to understand that he was afraid that he had somehow damaged me through his negative feelings towards me, causing me to become ill. Once we had explored the fantasy I agreed to tell him why I was taking the break. This necessitated us also facing reality: that I was choosing to leave him in order to undertake a piece of professional work that I enjoyed. This led to further work exploring what it meant to him that I could leave him in order to enjoy something that did not include him.

The transference relationship

The transference relationship is seen as the key to psychodynamic work. It starts before counsellor and client have actually met. For the client it begins at the point of deciding he wants help, for the counsellor when she gets the referral. By this I mean that both client and counsellor will have conscious and unconscious fantasies and expectations about the other in the relationship. This might sound rather fantastic – how can people have expectations of the relationship before they even meet? The following example highlights the extent to which expectations about the counselling relationship can be formed before the client comes into counselling.

Mark was a community psychiatric nurse who had suffered a period of depression some years previously; a colleague had recommended he contact me, but he did not follow up the recommendation. In the intervening years whenever he felt low he had fantasized about what it would be like to have counselling from me; he knew where I practised and at times drove past on his way to see his own clients. When he eventually came into counselling it was very quickly clear that he experienced me as someone who wasn't really there for him and who he felt neglected him. He didn't immediately tell me about how long he had taken to contact me, but when he did I understood that I had been his counsellor in fantasy for a number of years. During those years he wanted me to take care of him I hadn't been there to do so. So before he even started counselling his transference to me was to an absent and neglectful object. This then became part of his ongoing relationship with me.

Mark's experience is unusual in that most people who come into counselling have not waited so long to do so or had a particular person in mind, but it illustrates the extent to which the transference can exist without any experience of the actual person of the counsellor. The transference is based on early experience and fantasies associated with it: in Mark's case his mother had in reality been absent when he was young. She had been ill for much of his childhood and often in hospital, so he had a real experience of an absent object which was then re-created in the transference before he even entered counselling.

The first session is also very important in the establishment of the transference. This is particularly the case when the client has the potential for a strong negative transference.

> Following her first session with me Carol didn't attend her next appointment, leaving a message on my answering machine to say she wasn't coming back. Some while later I heard from a colleague that she hadn't wanted to continue with me because physically I reminded her of her mother, of whom she was quite terrified.

For the client the transference relationship can feel quite disturbing. Entering counselling usually precipitates an attachment crisis. By this I mean that the client would not have come into counselling unless there was a problem that he could not cope with alone, and he looks to the counsellor as someone who is stronger and more knowledgeable and who has the ability to take care of his needs. This stirs up early longings for, and fears of, closeness and intimacy and being looked after. The awakening of these transference feelings can take the client by surprise, and they are usually unwelcome, particularly if they are intense and accompanied by fantasies about the counsellor. Most adults do not welcome feeling needy of and dependent on someone else, and many are embarrassed by fantasies that might be childlike or sexual in nature.

Being the object of a client's transference can be quite demanding for the counsellor, to whom all sorts of attributes are ascribed. It requires a significant degree of abstinence to allow the transference to develop and not inhibit it, particularly when the client's transference doesn't fit with who the counsellor is or believes herself to be.

> A supervisee who was known for her sense of humour and enjoyment of life found it very difficult when a client insisted that she was dour and had no spark of fun about her. While she was aware that the client's father had been strict and forbidding, she found herself powerfully wanting to demonstrate to him that she did indeed have the capacity to laugh and enjoy herself. It was very difficult for her to accept his perception of her as transferential.

As counsellors we too have a transference to our clients. This is a combination of our general transference to all clients, and a particular transference to an individual client. Many of us who become counsellors have a history of difficulties in our own childhood, and a number have become carers at an early age. Clients in general might therefore elicit vicarious caring from us when they represent the needy part of ourselves that we seek to look after in the way we wish we had been cared for. Equally they might represent a damaged or ill parent whom we are trying to make better. Just as we ask about our clients, 'who am I in the transference for this person?' we also need to be aware of who our clients in general, or one in particular, represent for us.

Transference, then, is the bedrock of the therapeutic relationship for psychodynamic counsellors. We need to be aware of our own transferential needs so that we minimize the confusion between our clients and important objects from own past – hence the need for our own therapy or counselling. We also need to be aware of who we are to the client at any moment in the counselling session. This can change during a session, so that in different parts of one session we could come to represent different objects for the client, for example a parent, a sibling or a partner.

The countertransference

The way in which psychodynamic practitioners use their understanding of the countertransference is something that distinguishes psychodynamic practice from other forms of counselling. In other forms of counselling an appreciation of how she feels towards a client might guide the counsellor in her thinking about her client. Countertransference can therefore been seen as an advanced form of empathy. However, in psychodynamic counselling we use our countertransference to help us to understand our client's unconscious, in particular what he cannot bear to know himself and therefore projects into us. Being alive to one's countertransference is demanding as it involves allowing oneself to experience feelings that the client has found unbearable and has therefore cut himself off from. Quite often the psychodynamic counsellor's task can be to become a container for her client's intolerable feelings, and she has to bear them until the client is ready to acknowledge their existence, as illustrated in the next vignette.

> About a year into his counselling, there were times when I found it difficult to tolerate the feelings I experienced when I was with John. I suspected that Anne was having an affair with a man she'd met at the gym, but John himself was insistent that the relationship was no more than a friendship. This was despite the fact a friend had told John that Anne had been seen with the man at a restaurant when she said she was out with a girlfriend. He explained patiently to me that she needed to get out now that she was semi-retired, though he was concerned about the amount she was spending. I began to feel impotent, that there was no point in continuing the work as nothing I did would help John. One day I was feeling as though I should raise the question of ending counselling with him and I wondered if I wanted to act something out rather than understand it. I suspected that I was experiencing in the countertransference feelings that John was unable to bear – that he was impotent and unable to confront Anne about her new relationship for fear of losing her altogether. When eventually I was able to explore this hypothesis with him he confirmed that he was terrified that Anne was about to leave and that he would not be able to cope without her.

The extent to which a client communicates his internal world through the countertransference is understood as an indication of how disturbed he is at that given moment. The more the counsellor has to understand what is going on in a session through understanding her countertransference, the more likely it is that the client is operating in a primitive or early part of himself that is not accessible to consciousness. Those clients who communicate primarily through the countertransference are understood as being very disturbed, since they are unable to use other channels of communication such as verbal communication or behaviour. These clients may not be suitable for counselling but may need the skills of a psychotherapist or analyst. If she does work with such clients, the counsellor needs to ensure she has good supervision to prevent her from being overwhelmed and acting out the countertransference. In the example above, an attempt by me to end John's therapy would have been a form of countertransference acting out.

Gaining access to the unconscious

One of the things that many clients starting in psychodynamic counselling find difficult is that the counsellor does not structure the session for them. This stands in particularly strong contrast to some other forms of therapeutic interventions, for example IPT or CBT. So the psychodynamic counsellor may not be the first to speak in a session, unless it is clear that the client is unable to do so, and takes her lead from the client rather than suggesting a topic for discussion. This is done because one of the premises of psychodynamic work is that the client will have something that he needs to explore in the session, that he may not be consciously aware of. The psychodynamic counsellor's main task is to help the client towards saying what he needs to say. If she sets the agenda, or leads the conversation, the client may well be deterred from the task of discovering or discussing what is important for him.

Freud advocated the use of free association as a way of becoming in touch with these thoughts. Not infrequently, when they emerge as an idea that can be voiced, the client feels he has known about his thought or feeling all along, though he may never have expressed it before. Freud called this 'the unthought known'. Psychodynamic counsellors continue to use free association, by which I mean the client talks about whatever comes into his mind, trying not to censure it. This is easier said than done, as quite often what comes to mind might be difficult or embarrassing to say, and not make it past the client's internal censorship. Equally some clients dismiss what they are thinking if it does not immediately seem relevant to the concerns that brought them into counselling.

My own stance is that free association is often limited at the beginning of counselling and is an achievement, which comes later with trust, rather than a given. However, the counsellor encourages it from the beginning by not setting an agenda, by the way she responds to the client or by overtly asking the client to say whatever comes to mind. One of her tasks is to try to understand the sub-text of the story the client tells her in a session. This is rather like trying to understand the meaning of a dream. By understanding the sub-text the counsellor is trying to understand something of how the client's internal world is structured, the nature of the transference and the particular issue the client wants help with at that moment.

Another way of expanding the client's awareness of his unconscious is through the exploration of dreams. Jungian counsellors place a particular emphasis on dream work but it has an important role in other forms of psychodynamic counselling as well. Some counsellors will ask a client to describe a recent dream as part of the initial assessment. Others will wait and see if the client talks about dreams spontaneously.

The stages of counselling

Three stages of counselling have been identified: the beginning, middle and end. This applies whether the counselling is short- or long-term. Each stage involves particular tasks, though there is significant overlap between them. The initial stage involves the counsellor and client making an assessment of whether they want to work together, then building up a relationship in which the work of the counselling can be done. This stage can be quite protracted, lasting several months, particularly when a client has real difficulties in establishing trust. So the client might, for example, come to sessions but not really engage with the counsellor or the work of counselling. During this time the client may talk about his uncertainty about whether to continue, or may seem to idealize the counsellor, thus denying any negative feelings about counselling. It is during this stage that he is most likely to drop out if he does not make an emotional contact with her. During the sessions quite a lot of fire-fighting will probably go on, with the client focusing his emotional energies on the issues that brought him into counselling. Depending on the theoretical orientation of the counsellor and the needs of the client there might be less emphasis on the transference in this stage. If used, transference interpretations might focus on deepening the transference.

In the middle stage, trust has largely been established, and the client is feeling grateful to the counsellor for the help she has given him with the problems that brought him into counselling. The focus of the work begins to shift more towards an exploration of the transference and the client's internal world. This is when the bulk of the work will be done and in long-term counselling this stage can last from a few months to a number of years. The aims of counselling will often change as the client starts to understand his problems in a different way and take responsibility for bringing about the wished-for changes in his life.

> As John's relationship with Anne became more untenable he began to re-evaluate what he wanted from counselling. It had already evolved from (passively) wanting the pain to go away into (actively) wanting to be able to confront her with his unhappiness. However, as he faced up to the reality of her affair he began to realize how his dependence on her was based on a fear of being unable to function without her rather than a wish to be with her. In the transference relationship we explored the meaning of his need for me, and his fear that I too would abandon him, leaving him vulnerable and unable to care for himself.

At one level the ending is always present, from the end of the first session when the counsellor tells the client it is time to stop. But the final stage of counselling starts when client and counsellor agree that it is time to start working towards an ending. In this stage the major task is to say goodbye. This is often a very difficult time for the client. On the one hand he is ready to continue the work on his own and to leave counselling. At the same time leaving means giving up the intimacy involved in the relationship with his counsellor. Clients whose early lives have been characterized by loss can find it particularly difficult to say goodbye, especially if they have not developed other intimate relationships. The other task in this stage of counselling is to acknowledge what has been achieved and face the disappointment of what has not changed. Sometimes, as the ending draws close and the reality of saying goodbye becomes more acute, previously unexplored issues arise, leading to new work. Additionally, issues that had been worked through in the early or middle stages may reappear and need further attention. Generally speaking, the longer counselling has lasted the more time needs to be given to the ending. It is therefore important to ensure the client has enough time to undertake the tasks of ending and not avoid the pain associated with it by leaving prematurely. So, for example, someone who has had two years of counselling might need three months to work towards ending. Someone who is in short-term work of, say, 16 weeks would typically use the last four weeks to think about ending.

In the next chapter I shall look at some of the practical skills involved in putting these concepts into practice.

FIVE

Practical Skills in Psychodynamic Counselling

Psychodynamic counselling skills are built on a foundation of generic skills that are important in any counselling approach. These include a number that have been identified by person-centred counsellors, such as warmth, empathy and unconditional positive regard. By this I mean that the development of a working alliance in any counselling relationship requires that the counsellor has the capacity to feel warmth or caring towards her client, to be able to see the world through his eyes, and to be non-judgemental in her attitude towards him. She also needs a number of specific skills, such as being able to listen attentively and hold on to her client's story. Additionally, the skills of reflecting back and summarizing enable the client to hear what he has said put into a different language, which itself can often be very useful and encourage him to view what he said in a different way. Other skills include being able to say difficult things to the client, for example, helping him to face things about himself that he finds painful and would rather not confront. Good guides to these skills can be found in the Bibliography.

The specific psychodynamic skills that I want to look at in this chapter are: gaining informed consent; developing evenly suspended attention; listening to unconscious communication; making interpretations and structuring a session. Necessarily this will be a very brief introduction to an area about which much has been written, and again there are further recommendations for reading in the Bibliography. A word of caution is important here for those of you who want to work using the skills I am about to describe. Psychodynamic interventions are powerful tools, and thus have the potential to harm if used by an untrained practitioner who is not in her own counselling and supervision. To work ethically requires that you have your own psychodynamic counselling and supervision from trained psychodynamic practitioners.

Gaining informed consent

Gaining informed consent is a complex skill that requires a degree of sensitivity to the client's readiness to discuss the issues involved. As I discussed in Chapter 1, I feel that the best time to obtain initial consent is at the end of an assessment or 'trial' phase, which often means after approximately three to six sessions. However, if a client asks about the nature, risks and benefits of counselling before that, then they should be discussed.

One of the advantages of discussing consent after an assessment phase is that the counsellor should be better able to give some sort of explanation about what the client can expect on the basis of the experience he has already had and can understand. The process should also be facilitated by the therapeutic alliance, which will hopefully be sufficiently established to tolerate examination of consent issues. Gaining informed consent should include an explanation of the transference relationship; an understanding that psychodynamic counselling involves an exploration of the client's unconscious; and that psychodynamic counselling involves emotional disturbance and upset.

At this juncture the counsellor should also be in a position to indicate to the client some of the risks, difficulties and benefits he might anticipate from counselling. The counsellor should also explain to her client that it is not possible to entirely predict what is going to happen, how long counselling will take or how he will respond to it, and that the outcome is uncertain. In a sense the client who understands this is as fully informed as possible given our current state of knowledge and the inherent uncertainty about the process of counselling. Additionally, the counsellor should ensure that she is sufficiently familiar with other counselling approaches to be able to discuss them with her client. One way of facilitating this is to refer the client to literature that describes the basics of alternative approaches (for example other books in this series). Lastly, she needs to consider whether the client's difficulties are more suited to counselling or psychotherapy and be able to discuss the difference between them (see Chapter 6).

Finally, we should consider whether consent, having been given at the beginning of counselling, should continue to be sought throughout treatment. Again this presents a difficulty for psychodynamic counsellors about when and how to do this without interrupting or undermining the process of the psychodynamic endeavour unnecessarily. Continually seeking consent would be akin to pulling the seedling out of the plant-pot to make sure the roots are growing. To avoid this, ongoing consent is often taken as implicit, and this involves the dangers I discussed in Chapter 1. I am not advocating that consent should be sought at the beginning of each session or at a prescribed time interval without reference to the context in which it is being sought. However, we can and should ensure that we gain informed consent at the point where there are changes in the work, for example, if counsellor and client discuss a change in the frequency of sessions, if the work becomes more intense or risky or if either client or counsellor has concerns about the suitability of the approach.

Developing evenly suspended attention

As a fly on the wall watching a session, it might appear that the psychodynamic counsellor is just listening, and not doing very much. In fact she is working hard and doing a number of things at the same time. Most importantly, she is giving the client a quality of attention that has a profound influence on the atmosphere in the room. In turn this facilitates for the client a mental space in which he can develop the ability to become more thoughtful about himself and his internal world. One of the factors thought to bring about change in psychodynamic work is the experience of being really attended to and understood in this special way.

The counsellor moves between paying attention to what her client is saying and her own response. This involves a number of separate tasks.

Let's assume that the client is telling a story about something that has happened that week. My first task is to engage with the actual story and to be able to facilitate the client in telling it. At the same time I may also become aware of how this story links to other material the client has been discussing during this or in a previous session. While doing this I may start thinking about the story's possible hidden meaning. Does the story resonate with what I know about my client's inner world or life? I may also wonder about the story's transference implications, while at the same time monitoring my countertransference. What am I feeling and thinking in response to the story? Having identified this I need to consider whether it is likely that my feelings are the result of my own preoccupations, or, perhaps, useful information about my client's state of mind.

The aim in each session is to be aware both of conscious and unconscious material and communication and then convey what can be expressed to the client. In order to do this I need to develop a state of mind that Freud called 'evenly suspended attention' in which I am open to and move freely between my client's communication and my own state of mind. I must be able to tolerate the uncertainty of not knowing quite what is going on in the session, or what the client means at any one moment. So I have to be able to resist the need to be certain and provide answers; this in itself is a significant skill that new counsellors find quite difficult, since most of us in our adult lives strive towards knowing and abhor uncertainty. Bion famously went further than this and advocated that we should begin a session without preconceived ideas about what we expect from it. In other words, we cannot properly listen to what our client is saying to us if we arrive with our own agenda for the session. And it is not as straightforward as preventing him from telling us what he knows he wants to say. The objective of any session is to reach the 'unthought known' – to make conscious that which is not yet quite conscious. If we go in with our own agenda we are not available to hear the subtle nuances in someone's story that might lead to understanding what they are unconsciously trying to work with.

Acquiring the capacity to evenly suspend attention is a complex skill that develops over a period of time. The first and most important element in its development is the experience of a counsellor's own dynamic counselling or therapy. This is because it is only really possible to know what is meant by evenly suspended attention through experiencing it. The careful listening, the quality of respect for one's story, the attention to detail and the ability to hear that story on many different levels become internalized through the trainee counsellor's own experience of her personal counselling. Personal counselling also facilitates becoming aware of one's own feelings, internal world and unconscious motivation, a key factor in developing evenly suspended attention.

There are other aspects of the counsellor's training that also assist the development of evenly suspended attention. On some psychodynamic training courses trainees undertake a period of doing observations, sometimes of a baby or child, other times in a hospital ward or other workplace. While attending to what is going on, the trainee pays special attention to her own responses to what she observes. In my own training I found this particularly helpful because it was an opportunity to become aware of my feelings and thoughts without also having the responsibility for managing a therapeutic session. Supervision is also important. Counsellors in training are required to keep a detailed record (known as process notes) of what goes on between themselves and their clients, remembering as much of what was said and felt in the session as possible. Both the experience of writing up the notes and that of later discussing them with a supervisor encourage reflective capacity and evenly suspended attention in the trainee counsellor.

Listening to unconscious communication

One of the tasks in counselling is to try to understand the meaning behind your client's overt story or behaviour in the consulting room. To do this we need to develop an 'analytic ear', which involves listening to a story on many levels. We not only listen to the actual story but also to the meaning behind it. We need to be aware of how our clients (like all of us) try to protect themselves from unwanted feelings or knowledge, so when we listen we need to be attuned to how they might engage in self-deceit and resistance. This is not to say that we disbelieve what the client says or that we know better than him what he is really thinking. But it does recognize that, as human beings, we neither want to know nor feel that which is uncomfortable. We should take nothing for granted as we listen, to avoid either becoming seduced by what the client says, or assuming that we have a shared understanding of the meaning of what is said. Maintaining an analytic ear means at times suspending judgement about the actual truth of what the client is saying while accepting that at some level there is a truth in the underlying meaning behind his words.

So what do we do when we listen with an analytic ear and take nothing for granted? First, there is an attention to the detail that is unique to psychodynamic work; this applies both to what the client is conveying and to the shifts in the counselling relationship. Understanding a client's communication is a careful process, in which we attempt to make sense of everything he brings into the room with him. It involves being sensitive to the story he is actually telling, while asking questions in a way that does not undermine him. It also requires an awareness of the gaps and inconsistencies in his story, an attention to his body language and the silences in the session and paying attention to our own reaction to his communication. At the same time it is important to remember that making sense of the unconscious is a collaborative process and that constructing an understanding is only meaningful to the client if he has been part of it. It is not the job of the counsellor to pronounce on what the client is really thinking any more than the client should be a passive recipient of his counsellor's pronouncements.

One day, soon after acknowledging that Anne was having an affair, John arrived late. This was unusual for him. Even more unusually he didn't comment on his lateness. I wondered what this might signify. Had something important happened to him, or might he be upset with me about something? However, I waited to see what he brought to the session before saying anything. I felt that to comment straight away about his lateness could have been experienced as persecutory. He began the session by telling me that he was thinking about an incident that had just happened at work. One of his colleagues had been let down over holiday arrangements. He had been promised cover for a period of leave he had applied for, but then was told it wasn't possible after all. He was afraid of upsetting his wife if he changed their holiday dates, but if he insisted on taking the time off he feared upsetting his boss at work. John felt that the change in holiday arrangements was very unfair. This was a story that had a number of familiar themes to it; John often described situations where he too was caught between people who were pulling in different directions, but was rarely able to express his own anger at what was happening.

As I listened I found myself thinking about when I had given him my holiday dates two weeks earlier. He had commented that I had taken different holiday times from those the previous year. I hadn't had an opportunity to pursue the meaning of his comment at the time, but now I wondered whether there might be a link with the current story and the unusual start to the session. I started by acknowledging the content of his story, then I said to him that I wondered if his colleague's predicament might have resonated for him since he might have been quite inconvenienced by the change to my holiday dates from last year. He said it was his own fault for not checking with me first. I then suggested that he might have experienced me as being unreasonable in making the change to my holiday dates. He then acknowledged that he had tried to change his holiday times to fit in with mine, but had been unable to do so, so his break from counselling would be extended if he were to take a holiday at the time he had planned. I then suggested that he might be quite angry about the change of time, and wondered if his late arrival might have been the result of a conflict inside him about telling me of his disappointment with me. John agreed, and said he had been quite upset with me but hadn't known how to talk about it. He was frightened that if he complained I would be angry and not want to see him any more.

In listening to John's story I was very mindful of why he might be choosing to tell me this story rather than any other. After all, there is limited time in any session and therefore I treated everything that happened and everything John said as significant. The way in which he used this session was unusual because he arrived late and then did not comment on the fact he had done so. This immediately alerted me to the probability that there was something he might find difficult to talk to me about. As I listened to his story I needed to be aware of any feelings or thoughts I might have in relation to it. However, because communication happens at a number of different levels and John's unconscious is by definition unknown, I could not be sure I had understood what he was trying to communicate; I could only hypothesize.

You will notice that when I described my responses to John that I 'suggested' or 'wondered' about what might be going on. There are two reasons for doing this. The first is that I may well have been wrong. If the client finds what we say helpful, he is likely to indicate this by what he says in response. John's responses to my intervention suggested that my hypothesis was correct. However, by being tentative I also offer him the opportunity to disagree with me and for us then to explore alternative understandings. The second reason for offering my thoughts as a hypothesis is to do with the power I have as a counsellor. If I say something very definitively it can make it much more difficult for my client to disagree with me. It may also make him feel as though I know what's going on in his mind better than he; perhaps even that I can read his mind. This can be harmful, particularly to those clients who do not have a very strong sense of their own identity.

When a client brings up a dream we know that he is telling us something of his unconscious preoccupations. Most people do not remember most of their dreams. So I am interested in why this dream has been remembered and why the client has chosen to talk about it in the session. When the story of the dream has been told I want to know what the client makes of the dream; I want to know what his thoughts and associations are. An association is a thought or feeling that comes to the client in response to something he or his counsellor has said. It often comes in the form of a story of a past or current event which the client and counsellor together try to make sense of. Counsellors have different ways of asking their clients for associations. Some will ask directly, 'what do you think the dream was about?', while others will wait and see what the client talks about next and assumes that there is a link with the dream. Some practitioners will go as far as to say that everything else that the client does or says in the session is an association to the dream.

> Tania had been coming to counselling for just a few weeks. She was describing how she had always been popular with her peers and had been at the centre of the 'in-crowd' at a school where social competition was particularly strong. As she did so she conveyed a degree of anxiety that was at odds with the story she was telling. I commented that being the centre of the in-crowd might have been quite a strain and that she might have been quite anxious about whether she could maintain her popularity. 'It never felt that way,' she said. She then remembered a dream she had had a few nights previously. 'I was at the airport in the queue to check in. I was late for the flight and I was anxious I was going to miss it. Then suddenly all these friends I was supposed to be travelling with arrived and went to the front of the queue. They didn't seem to notice me. By the time they'd been booked in I'd missed my flight and they'd all left without me.' I commented to her that in her dream she wasn't at the centre of her group of friends, and in fact was left behind. She then said that when she was first at the school she had felt very left out because she was from a less affluent part of the town than the other children. She paused, and then said, 'You know, I'd never thought about it like this before, but I think I was always frightened that, unless I was at the centre of the crowd, one day they'd all turn on me.'

Tania tells me about her dream as an association to her own thoughts about being popular at school and my comment that maintaining her popularity might have been quite a strain for her. Her unconscious anxiety about not being wanted is conveyed vividly in her dream and as she begins to think about the content of her dream becomes aware of just how anxious she actually was about her position in relation to her peers. As we explored her associations further, Tania was able to begin to think about her fear that she was not lovable, and that unless she pleased everyone no one would want her. It is through this attention to detail as well as by listening at a number of levels that unconscious material is accessed.

Making interpretations

As discussed previously, in the course of a session the counsellor can represent one of a number of important objects for her client. Transference interpretations are those that refer specifically to the client's relationship to his counsellor and who she represents for him at that moment. Extra-transference interpretations involve understanding the links between events, thoughts, feelings or behaviour that are not directly to do with the relationship between the client and counsellor. Psychodynamic counsellors will use both types of interpretation.

> Richard was a trainee counsellor who was in counselling with Frank. Richard had come to a session one day very upset that a fellow trainee, Gill, had started counselling with someone who, it was rumoured, had poor personal/professional boundaries. Richard had not known what to say to Gill, because he didn't want to upset her as she clearly liked her new counsellor, but at the same time he was very worried that she might be vulnerable to him abusing his power as her counsellor. Richard was aware that Frank knew the counsellor because they belonged to the same counselling organization. He found it difficult to believe Frank was unaware of this man's reputation. Richard had, as a child, been abused by a scout-master and Frank was aware of how sensitive he was to behaviour he perceived as an abuse of power. In the session Frank had helped Richard to recognize his impotence in the face of Gill's choice and to further explore his own fury about the abuse he had suffered as a child. He also interpreted to Richard that he was angry with him because, like Richard's mother, who had not protected him from abuse by the scout-master, Frank had not taken any steps to protect vulnerable trainees from a potentially abusive situation.

In this vignette Frank makes both types of interpretation. First, he makes extra-transference interpretations about Richard's impotence in the face of Gill's decision as well as about his own experience of being abused as a child. Frank addresses the transferential aspects of the story by hypothesizing that Richard is angry with him because he has not protected someone who is vulnerable from a person who might abuse her. In fact we might say that at that moment in the transference Frank has become the mother who failed to protect her child from abuse. In making this interpretation Frank makes a link between the current situation (Richard's anger that his friend will be abused), the past (Richard's anger at his mother for not protecting him from abuse as a

Practical Skills in Psychodynamic Counselling **81**

child) and the transference relationship (Richard's anger with Frank for not protecting someone who is vulnerable to abuse). This three-way link of past, present and the relationship with the counsellor is called the Triangle of Person.

When interpreting we need to be careful that we don't avoid what the client is most concerned with at that moment. So, for example, if a client is very upset by something in his own life that he is working hard to face, it may not be helpful to make a transference interpretation. To do so may dilute the power of what he is feeling about a past or present hurt and make him feel he is not being heard. Conversely, if a client is really upset with his counsellor it is not always helpful to make a link with the client's past, even though it may be very clear that his distress has links to his past history. It is often uncomfortable for both client and counsellor to work with the issues that are causing most distress; it can be particularly difficult for the counsellor to keep interpreting in the transference when she is feeling attacked by her client.

Psychodynamic practitioners make transference interpretations in different ways. Many will advocate starting at the point that feels least threatening for the client, particularly if the relationship is new, or the work has moved into a new area. You will notice in the vignettes that I don't immediately interpret the transferential aspects of the material. It can be appropriate to do so with a client whom we know well and who has been in counselling for some time. However, it is usually more acceptable to the client if a transference interpretation is gradually built up to so that it is not experienced as coming out of the blue.

The timing of an interpretation is crucial to its effectiveness. A poorly timed interpretation might be correct, but it is of no use to the client if it is experienced as intrusive or overwhelming. A badly timed but correct interpretation can even do harm if it increases a client's defensiveness about an area of sensitivity that he is not yet ready to think about. A correct and well-timed interpretation requires us to take into account the client's perspective: it is important to think about how our interpretation will impact on him and imagine what it might be like to be him receiving it. An interpretation that is helpful will bring forth more material from the client and this in itself can be confirmatory of the accuracy of the interpretation. When a counselling couple is working well the counsellor may be ready to make the transference interpretation just before the client gets there himself; indeed, the client may make all or part of the interpretation himself.

The other kind of interpretation that can be made from the therapeutic relationship is a countertransference interpretation. Using one's countertransference as the basis for understanding a client is something that requires a high level of skill, and is one of the most difficult things to do well in psychodynamic work. A countertransference interpretation does not make direct reference to what the counsellor herself is feeling. Instead she uses what she thinks has been projected into her to try to understand what the client might not be able to face himself.

> Now that John knew Anne was having an affair he was trying to decide what to do. He had not yet confronted her and was considering doing so the following weekend. He was also wondering whether to contact a solicitor to discuss his legal position. He spoke in a very practical way and seemed quite remote from what he was talking about, but I began to experience a terrible feeling of emptiness and loss. Eventually, after considering my own state of mind and deciding these feelings were not consonant with my own current preoccupations, I ventured the following interpretation. 'You're thinking very carefully about the practical consequences of facing Anne with what you now know about her affair, but I wonder whether it might be more difficult to face the possible emotional consequences of doing so.' 'I don't think I can even bear to think about that at the moment,' he replied. Some time later in the session he began to talk about a friend of his whose wife had recently left him. The friend had almost immediately begun another relationship and John felt he was avoiding the pain of losing his wife. 'I wonder whether you too are finding it very difficult to face how alone and lost you might feel if you separate from Anne,' I said.

You will notice that I approached the countertransference interpretation carefully. Initially John did not want to pursue my offer to think about what he might be feeling about the consequences of facing Anne with his knowledge of her affair. It was only after he told me the story of his friend's difficulty in dealing with his loss that I felt he had given me permission to interpret more directly from my countertransference. To have made an initial interpretation about his feelings of loss and emptiness would have felt too threatening, given that he was so cut off from these feelings earlier in the session.

The structure of a session

What the client says at the beginning of a session might well hold a clue about the conscious, preconscious or unconscious preoccupations he brings with him; so it is always important to take note of any comments he makes on the way to the consulting room.

> As he arrived following an Easter break, John commented on some changes that I had made to my waiting room. Later in the session he told a story of a teacher who was very unreliable – she was forever changing her mind about what she wanted from her pupils. I wondered whether the changes in my waiting room had accessed fears in John about my reliability at a time when he badly needed me to be dependable and predictable. When I made an interpretation to this effect he confirmed that, on seeing my waiting room, he had wondered what other changes I might want to make; eventually he said he feared I might also want to change the clients I see, including him.

Most psychodynamic counsellors will see their clients once a week. So when the client arrives for his session he may need time to adjust to being back in the counselling relationship and talking about his inner world. The beginning of the session is likely to be about the client's current preoccupations, and he may well start the session by telling his counsellor about what has happened since they last met. Carefully concentrating with evenly suspended attention the counsellor will listen for the underlying message his story may convey and begin to make links and interpretations.

Throughout the session the counsellor will be listening for themes in what her client is talking about, and thinking about how they relate to what she knows of him. She will make links and interpretations that deepen his emotional engagement with the feelings attached to the memories and associations that unfold. She will also help him gain a greater understanding of what he brings. The counsellor's work involves entering the client's world and becoming involved in his story and then standing back and taking an objective view of what he is saying and the interaction between them. She will make this transition several times during the session. During the middle stage of the session the client (and sometimes the counsellor too) may enter a state the Jungians call 'child time'. This involves losing a sense of time in the session in the way children do when they are playing. It is the counsellor's responsibility to hold the time boundary and to be aware that the end of the session is approaching.

Quite often the deepest understanding will come quite near the end of the session when the client is able to allow the unthought known to be thought and known about. However, ideally the end of the session should not come as too much of a shock to the client. If the client has been working with deep feelings the counsellor should begin to prepare for the end of the session, for example by making extra-transference interpretations to bring a greater sense of reality into the room. Occasionally it is helpful to give a deeply upset client warning a few minutes before the end that the session is about to finish. Once out of the session the client will have to contain his feelings himself. Often inexperienced counsellors are afraid of allowing too much emotion in the session for fear that the client will be unable to contain it once the session is finished. While it is important that clients are not suddenly dropped at the end of a session, some of this fear is associated with the counsellor's own anxiety that she might damage her client. Such concerns about causing damage should be explored in the counsellor's own personal counselling.

SIX
Beyond Theory and Practice

In this chapter I want to think beyond theory and practice to look at the contextual frame in which psychodynamic counselling exists. The context is something that is in a constant state of development, as changes in society face psychodynamic practice with ongoing challenges in areas such as ethics and supervision. At the same time, changes in our understanding of what causes psychological difficulties and brings about change require us to rework both theory and practice. But I want to start by looking at the counsellor who offers her client counselling and the journey she needs to make in order to be able to do so.

The importance of personal counselling for counsellors

A few years ago Bollas, a psychoanalyst, made a strong argument for the importance of personal counselling when he stated that we can only find our patient (the person we're working with) if we have first found the patient in ourselves. His proposal indicates the importance of recognizing that, like our clients, counsellors also have emotional vulnerabilities, internal conflicts and developmental deficits. In order to work well, we need to address these areas before seeking to help others. While this holds true for counsellors working in all models, it is particularly the case for psychodynamic counsellors whose work is embedded in deepening the transference relationship and working with the unconscious meaning of that relationship. Because we work in this way we are particularly vulnerable to bringing our own unprocessed issues into the counselling relationship.

Counsellors who do not find the patient in themselves cannot properly register the experience of their clients, and may have a difficulty in appropriately identifying with them, becoming either over-involved, or too detached and therefore too distant. Alternatively, they can struggle to hold therapeutic boundaries, or recognize those clients that they are not equipped to work with or who can't be helped. Lastly, the counsellor may also find it hard to recognize when her own emotional difficulties mean that she is no longer fit to practise and needs to stop work for a period of time.

A further reason for embarking on one's own counselling is that it is instructive to know first hand what it is like to be in the client's rather than the counsellor's chair. For example, we are less likely to be frightened of a client's dependency needs if we ourselves have had such feelings about our own counsellor. It can be enormously helpful for us to know for ourselves as counsellors what it is like to seek help when in crisis. Furthermore, counsellors who are profoundly helped by their own experience of receiving counselling often demonstrate particularly well-developed skills of attunement and sensitivity in their work.

It is also important that we understand why we have chosen counselling as a career, and our own counselling creates the opportunity to make that discovery. Most people embark on a counselling career out of a wish to help others, however imprecisely they understand that wish. But it is essential that, as counsellors, we have a deeper understanding of why we have chosen to help other people in this particular way, since our unconscious motivation to do so impacts on our attitude towards and relationship with our clients.

Below are some of the reasons why people want to become counsellors, and the difficulties that can arise if they do not recognize and work with those reasons:

- A wish to repair the wounds in themselves resulting from unmet needs or conflicts in their developmental history (unrecognized this can lead to

counsellor or client acting out in an attempt to recreate a situation that addresses the counsellor's developmental needs or conflicts).
- The wish to repair a member or members of their family whose damage has impacted on them (unrecognized this can lead to heroic attempts to help someone beyond the counsellor's level of competency, and an associated difficulty in knowing when to refer on).
- Difficulty in having intimate relationships with other people unless they are in a helping role towards them (unrecognized this can lead to abuse of the counsellor's position of power by making the client feel more helpless and dependent than he is so that counselling is prolonged, thus maintaining a level of emotional intimacy with the counsellor).
- Getting their own needs for caring met vicariously by caring for other people (unrecognized this can make it difficult for the counsellor to help clients towards independence and health, or she may take on too many clients if the need to get care for herself this way becomes compulsive).

These reasons are nearly always unconscious and rarely understood before the counsellor has done sufficient work in her own counselling. Unless they are so much part of her characterological make-up that they cannot be worked with, they are not of themselves a bar to becoming a counsellor. However, they do need to be understood and worked with and doing so is an important part of counsellors' personal and professional development.

Lastly, the counsellor's own counselling offers her the opportunity to experience a senior member of the profession at work in a way that is not otherwise available in psychodynamic work. Because psychodynamic practitioners do not routinely observe one another either live or through video, there are limited opportunities to find out how someone else works as a means of learning new skills. Being in counselling herself may be the trainee counsellor's only exposure to a live experience of how certain aspects of therapeutic work are undertaken, for example how a holding environment is achieved. Thus, one's own counselling becomes an important contribution to the implicit learning about 'how to' that helps one develop as a counsellor. Many counsellors, when struggling with a difficult therapeutic dilemma, think back on how their own counsellor managed similar situations with them and have found it helpful in deciding what to do. This can feel immensely reassuring, particularly in the early years after qualifying. At the same time the counsellor in training has the opportunity to decide what she would not take from her counsellor's way of working into her own practice, and therefore what she would not do with her own clients. However, while there are clear advantages to experiencing how someone else 'does' counselling, I am definitely not advocating that counsellors in training primarily go through their own counselling as a means to find out 'how to do it'. Treating your own counselling primarily as an apprenticeship can become a defence against being properly helped. Those who do that very often don't get as much help from their counselling as they could, and usually need.

How does the experience of psychodynamic counselling compare to other approaches?

One of the drivers regarding the availability of psychological therapies has been the agenda of giving clients choice about the approach they engage in, in recognition of the fact that 'one size does not fit all'. In the UK, within the public health sector the choice for individual short-term therapy includes IPT, CBT, Cognitive Analytical Therapy (CAT) and person-centred as well as psychodynamic approaches. The research evidence now strongly indicates two things: first, in short-term work the therapeutic alliance between counsellor and client is the most important single determinant of outcome, no matter which approach is adopted. Secondly, no one psychotherapy model is superior in reducing the symptoms of psychological distress, but clients' belief in the efficacy of a model does have an impact on how helpful they find it. So on what basis might clients choose the psychodynamic approach over others when seeking help?

Given the breadth of my training I am often asked to assess clients who do not know what kind of help they prefer. It has to be taken as a given that they are all in psychological distress and to some extent are experiencing symptoms of that distress which they are seeking to alleviate. However, how they want to approach overcoming their difficulties varies enormously. Some people very clearly want an approach that addresses current functioning and that is active in the sense of having homework assignments and requires deliberately practising new skills; these are people who would be better served by CBT or perhaps IPT. Others may want to explore their feelings about a circumscribed current event and would be happier using a person-centred approach.

Those who eventually enter either short- or long-term psychodynamic counselling often do so because, as well as symptom relief, they are seeking to understand themselves better; are wondering why they keep repeating relationship or other life patterns in an unsatisfactory way; are disturbed by events or relationships in their past which they recognize impact on their present functioning; or want to explore issues from their past in their own right. Sometimes they have tried other approaches and felt they have not gone 'far enough' and want to think more deeply about the problems troubling them. Other times they have previously had a successful experience of another therapeutic approach but have been unable to manage their symptoms when problems reoccur; these clients often wish to explore the issues underlying their distress in an effort to help them put into practice the techniques they have learned and found useful in the previous model.

Clients entering long-term psychodynamic counselling need to accept that symptom relief is likely to come more slowly than in symptom-focused therapies like CBT. This is because in the psychodynamic approach the primary vehicle for change is the therapeutic relationship and through it a change in the client's internal relationship to himself. It takes time for the counsellor to get to know her client and for the client to come to trust the counsellor at the deep level required for such change to take place. Someone who is impatient for change, or whose focus is on symptom relief, will be frustrated by a psychodynamic approach. Likewise if a client is very dismissive of relationships he may not find the psychodynamic approach conducive. It is less of a problem if the client is dismissive of the impact of his early experience on his current functioning, as often such clients begin to develop a curiosity about their early life as they begin to think about repeated patterns in their current life.

Although psychodynamic work traditionally took place over an extended period of time, there is also substantial experience in offering different short-term psychodynamic interventions. These interventions have two things in common. First, unlike in long-term psychodynamic practice, they select a focus for the work, which might be a problematic relationship or a 'core conflict' that the client is struggling with (for example a conflict around the fear of getting close to people). Secondly, they tend to focus on the transference relationship more explicitly from the beginning, whereas in longer-term work it is allowed to develop more slowly. The experience for the client in short-term work is that the psychodynamic counsellor works in a much more active way, and maintains the focus of the work. However, as in longer-term psychodynamic counselling, the aim of the work is to bring about change in the client's relationships or the core conflict that brought him into treatment and through that a change in his symptoms.

There is an emphasis in short-term psychodynamic counselling in conducting a thorough assessment. This increases the chance that when a focus for the work is agreed it is both meaningful to the client and makes sense in terms of formulating his difficulties, so that the work can be undertaken at a faster pace. It is important to emphasize that short-term interventions are not suitable for all clients (if they were we would have no need of longer-term work!). It is particularly suited to those clients who have a reasonably strong ego, and who are coping with issues that are more associated with conflict, than those whose ego is damaged through early neglect or trauma who need the opportunity to create a relationship of trust over a longer period of time.

This focus on the transference distinguishes short-term psychodynamic counselling from psychodynamically informed work, which is also often short-term, but here the transference is noted and used to inform how counselling proceeds rather than directly interpreted. This is when psychodynamic work can be an appropriate short-term intervention for people who have experienced early neglect or trauma and who consequently have a poorly developed sense of self. By not deepening the transference, such clients can be helped to understand their difficulties without their fragile ego being overwhelmed by the intensity of the relationship with their counsellor.

Is there a difference between psychodynamic counselling and psychodynamic therapy?

If I were to watch a video of a counsellor and a psychotherapist working in a psychodynamic model with a client in once-a-week treatment, I might find it difficult to tell you who was the counsellor and who the psychotherapist. There would probably be a greater difference in the style and quality of work within groups of counsellors and groups of psychotherapists than between the two. So are there any real differences between the two approaches or is it just a question of semantics? Some would argue that there are very few, that we are all working from the same theory base and use the same concepts and skills. Others argue that there are significant differences, that one approach is superior to the other. In my opinion, there is a significant overlap between counselling and psychotherapy and good practitioners of each will work in very similar ways. Nevertheless, there are some differences and I think it is important to acknowledge them. The commonalities lie in the fact that they both adhere to the basic requirements of any psychodynamic training: that trainees have their own counselling or therapy, that they undertake supervised practice with clients and learn about psychodynamic theory. Likewise, in practice the transference relationship is at the centre of the work for all psychodynamic practitioners. The major differences lie in the way that counsellors and psychotherapists are trained and the intensity of work they can consequently undertake.

All psychodynamic training courses require trainees to have a certain amount of personal counselling or therapy while training. Counsellors are usually required to have once-a-week counselling, sometimes this is open-ended or it might be for a minimum number of sessions. Psychotherapy courses require their trainees to see their own therapist two or three times a week throughout their training, which may last four or more years. Similarly counsellors in training usually see their clients once a week, whereas psychotherapists have to see theirs two or three times a week, depending on the course.

Not uncommonly, psychotherapists give their clients the choice between sitting in a chair and lying on a couch, and some psychotherapy trainings expect trainees to use a couch both for their own personal therapy and for their training clients. Using a couch can evoke stereotypical ideas of psychoanalysis. Freud originally used a couch when he hypnotized his patients in the early days of his work, but continued to do so when he stopped using hypnosis because he felt it aided the development of the transference. The analyst, sitting out of sight behind the patient, could become a 'blank screen' onto which the patient could project his childhood conflicts and fantasies. Today we no longer think of psychotherapists as blank screens. However, many psychotherapists still use a couch because it helps both the client and the therapist be more in touch with unconscious processes. Partly this is because someone who is prone is more able to access his inner feelings; there is an inevitable regression that occurs when lying down. But also there is a distraction from the unconscious when two people face each other because each is watching for and reacts to the social cues of the other. This might inhibit the deeper work that is being attempted in a more intense therapy.

Thus, psychotherapists are trained to work more intensively with their clients than counsellors in a number of ways. Some people will use this as an argument that psychotherapists are therefore better qualified because they have had a more intensive training. Equally it could be argued that counsellors, who are trained to work with people on a weekly basis, are better trained to do so than psychotherapists who are not. Once trained, psychotherapists tend to see their clients more intensively over longer periods than do counsellors and will see clients with longer-term or more intractable problems. However, there is considerable overlap here, and some counsellors will mostly work long term, while some psychotherapists will offer mostly short-term work.

I started this section by saying that it might be difficult to tell a counsellor from a therapist if both were conducting weekly sessions. However, there are differences that are real. If you want to work seeing clients once a week or want once-a-week treatment yourself, the differences between counsellors and psychotherapists are very difficult to quantify. It is much more important that you find the right person for you, whatever her qualifications. The differences become more obvious if you are interested in more intensive work, for yourself as a client or to train in a more intensive method. If this is the case you will need to consider psychotherapy.

What's it like being a psychodynamic counsellor?

Like any profession, counselling has its rewards and its shortcomings. Perhaps one testament to the intrinsic rewards of the work is that once people start working as counsellors they tend to continue. This perhaps has something to do with the fact that many people enter the profession later as part of a career or life change. The fact that most people pay for their own training may also ensure that only those who are committed continue.

Being a psychodynamic counsellor is challenging, stimulating and rewarding on a number of levels. Perhaps the biggest challenge is emotional. Working psychodynamically requires the counsellor to develop a capacity to become available to the unconscious needs and fantasies of her clients. This regular exposure to other people's distress and their projections is draining, and often at the end of a session the psychodynamic counsellor is left with difficult feelings to process. It is also demanding to sustain analytic neutrality and abstinence in the face of continual invitations (explicit and implicit) to abandon that neutrality and engage in a different type of relationship. At some time or another most counsellors will also have to cope with a client who is a suicide risk or even one who makes a successful suicide attempt, with the associated feelings of responsibility or failure. Because of the strains imposed by the work, the British Association of Counselling and Psychotherapy (BACP) lays down guidelines about the maximum number of clients that should be seen in a day.

Psychodynamic work is also very stimulating. In the work with my clients I often feel as though I am functioning at the limits of my ability, both emotionally and intellectually. I am rarely bored in my work, and if I am that in itself becomes something for me to wonder about, as it usually indicates something important is happening between my client and me. Additionally, psychodynamic ideas are intellectually challenging and offer a frame not only for understanding our clients and ourselves, but also how organizations and wider society function.

Ultimately psychodynamic counselling is very rewarding work. It is a huge privilege and very humbling to be invited in to another person's inner world and to share his or her life in this way. To enter into deep relationships with people and contribute in a positive way to their lives, to know that the changes in a client are partly a function of your skill and expertise, is deeply satisfying. With that satisfaction comes another of the demands. Having made relationships with our clients they and we then have to say goodbye. The breaking of these, often deep, bonds creates an emotional strain on the counsellor who has to mourn the loss of a series of intimate relationships. The nature of the relationship with our clients is not replicated in other relationships outside the consulting room, however intimate they are in other ways. So the loss of that intimacy with a longstanding client is a real loss for the counsellor too. And, as Winnicott once observed, the paradox is that in the final stages of counselling, as we prepare to say goodbye, our relationships with our clients probably become more enjoyable as we become less concerned for them.

Ethical practice

Ethical practice is built on the values that we hold both as professionals and as members of society. As values in society change, for example the move towards a greater degree of openness and accountability, the practice and ethics of counselling has to reflect those changes. Examples include keeping personal data and informing clients of their rights, and what to expect in counselling. This poses particular challenges for psychodynamic counsellors since some of the requirements of modern ethical practice can be experienced as running counter to good psychodynamic practice. I have already addressed the issue of informed consent, but another difficult area for psychodynamic practice is the requirement to keep accurate records of sessions in the knowledge that they can be requested by a third party. Practitioners have to keep in mind both the need to represent what occurred in the session, and that that their notes often describe material that reflects the client's psychic reality rather than external reality, and unconscious processes rather than historical truth. If session notes are required by a third party (for example a solicitor) counsellors need to be aware that the notes are vulnerable to misinterpretation unless the person reading them has a good understanding of unconscious processes. The potential for the disclosure of notes causing harm to a client has, at times, been successfully used as an argument for withholding notes from third parties when counsellors are unhappy about the way in which the notes could be misinterpreted. If a client gives consent to his notes being sent to a solicitor it can be important that he read his notes before they are sent. Once he has read them the counsellor will be in a better position to ensure that his consent really is informed.

Each organization that registers psychological practitioners has guidelines about ethical practice. The BACP sets out guidelines to good practice based on its principles of counselling and psychotherapy such as trust, beneficence, non-maleficence and justice. It also sets out the personal moral qualities that it requires of its practitioners, such as empathy, respect and competence. The BACP's guidance is detailed and comprehensive, but practitioners should be familiar not only with their own organization's code of practice, but how recent changes in legislation and society's attitudes affect their responsibilities to clients, colleagues and the profession. It is therefore helpful to be aware of national frameworks or legislation, for example in the UK the Data

Protection Act 1998 gives clear guidelines around keeping records confidential; the Children Act 2004 delineates under what circumstances client confidentiality should be broken to protect the welfare of children; and the Health Professions Council (HPC) lays out standards of conduct and ethics which supersedes individual organizations' guidelines for those who are registered with it.

The HPC requires that practitioners:

- Act in the best interests of their clients
- Respect clients' confidentiality
- Inform regulators of any important information about their own conduct and competence
- Keep their professional knowledge and skills up to date
- Act within the limits of their knowledge, skills and experience and, if necessary refer on to another practitioner
- Keep accurate records.

Although some guidelines are detailed, all essentially provide a framework for practice rather than a prescription for every situation a practitioner might encounter. Within that framework there is scope for considerable interpretation and professional judgement. It is therefore important to bear in mind that we all have the capacity to deceive ourselves into thinking we are acting correctly when we are not. This is why it is so important to take our work to supervision and to be honest about what we are doing.

The place of supervision in psychodynamic counselling

All psychodynamic counsellors are required to access supervision, whether they are in training or are very senior members of the profession. Supervision is important for a number of reasons: first, being able to use supervision has been identified as a necessary competency for counsellors working in all therapeutic models; secondly, research has demonstrated that the quality of counsellors' therapeutic work is related to the quality of the supervision they receive; lastly, good supervision after qualification acts as a protection against becoming burnt out and acting unethically. Supervision is also a requirement for registration with professional bodies and a part of clinical governance within the organizations in which counsellors work. Being able to use supervision well is important to counsellors' professional lives, since much of their ongoing professional development is transmitted through it.

Supervision has a number of purposes:

- *Education:* Develops the counsellor's skills, understanding and abilities, and is achieved through reflection on and exploration of her client work.
- *Support:* Gives the counsellor time and space in which to become aware of how she has been affected by her work and deal with any consequent reactions. It is intended to help her manage her clients' projections and to process any emotions stimulated from her own past. Ultimately it is aimed at preventing both acting out and burning out. It is the area where therapy and supervision can overlap (see below).
- *Quality control:* Which can involve: identifying training needs; identifying 'blind spots' or where personal vulnerabilities or prejudices interfere with the counsellor's work; ensuring that ethical standards are maintained; ensuring the standards set by the organization or governing body are maintained.

Although supervision is essential to help counsellors cope with their work, it also ranks as one of the major stressors for trainee counsellors and a difficult supervisory relationship can be problematic even for experienced counsellors. One of the ways of reducing stress is to ensure that the supervisory alliance is paid attention to, and it is important to remember that being supervised is not a passive process. One of the ways counsellors can ensure supervision is used effectively is through thinking clearly about their supervisory needs and setting up a supervisory contract, established through discussion between the counsellor and her supervisor. This might include how material is presented in supervision, how frequently supervisor and counsellor meet, whether contact is available outside supervision times, being clear about each other's expectations of supervision and how any problems in the supervisory relationship are addressed. It is also important to discuss the boundary between counselling and supervision, since supervisees sometimes get help for themselves through the process of discussing their work with their supervisor, particularly when that work touches on issues that are important to them personally.

This stance requires that the counsellor takes some responsibility for the relationship with her supervisor, and the quality of the supervision she receives. In psychodynamic supervision doing so can be a significant challenge. There is an inherently hierarchical apprentice model in psychodynamic practice, which can make it difficult to be assertive about one's needs in supervision. However, it is important for counsellors to get the best out of supervision in order to facilitate their professional growth. Doing so may necessitate confronting some of these inherent difficulties.

At the beginning of their career, counsellors are well advised to find someone whose theoretical orientation is the same as that of their own counsellor, since it can be confusing to experience two very different viewpoints about technique or theory early on. The trainee's supervisor and counsellor in effect constitute a parental couple. If they advocate different approaches (for example supervision from a Jungian and counselling with a Freudian), the trainee can become confused about what constitutes 'correct' behaviour in her work, potentially leading to a delay in her development.

Does psychodynamic counselling work?

At the end of his counselling John had left Anne and had moved into rented accommodation. He had done a lot of work in mourning the loss of his marriage. However, he had also recognized how, through his marriage, he had remained dependent on a maternal figure from whom he was unable to separate. He realized that his fear of losing Anne had prevented him from becoming or doing anything that might upset her.

> The compromises he had had to make to achieve this had been at the expense of his own sense of self. The increase in his self-confidence that came from facing his difficulties enabled him to make a successful application for promotion at work. This meant moving away from the area, no longer living near his parents and finishing his counselling with me. He was both fearful and excited by this. Most importantly, he wanted to try being independent.
>
> Through the relationship with me he had learned that he could grow from dependence to greater independence, that he could be angry and difficult and still be wanted. He had discovered me not only as a transference figure but as a new object, with whom he could have a different and more honest relationship. There were areas of his life that still concerned him. In particular he had not made a new relationship, which meant that he had not had the opportunity to discover whether his problems with Anne would re-emerge with another partner. We both recognized he may need further help if he did begin another relationship.

Like most people who undertake long-term counselling, John was ending feeling a mixture of pleasure about what had been achieved and regrets about what had not been possible. Accepting the limitations of what can be changed is an important part of working towards the ending in any counselling relationship. My task as his counsellor was to help him bear his disappointment in what we had not achieved as well as to share in his pleasure about what we had. Importantly, I also needed to be able to help John to mourn the loss of our relationship while at the same time helping him to leave me. Each counselling relationship is unique and, even if he were to seek counselling in the future, our relationship could not be replicated. Furthermore, the process of mourning the loss of the counselling relationship with me would, in itself, be helpful to him in the future when he needed to mourn other losses.

Most of us who have had a period of psychodynamic counselling or therapy will testify to the benefits it has brought to our mental health and our relationships. Those benefits can include improvement to or changes in important relationships so that those relationships are more meaningful and satisfactory; greater self-knowledge and insight so that we are more aware of what motivates us and how we impact on other people; a more benign superego so that we feel more at ease with ourselves and are less self-punishing and more understanding of our vulnerabilities; a more robust ego, or sense of self, so we are more able to manage life's knocks without resorting to unhelpful defences; and relief from distressing psychological symptoms such as low self-esteem or feelings of anxiety so that we are freer to live life without being hampered by them. It is this whole picture of change that is so valued by those who seek help through psychodynamic approaches.

These important changes in psychological functioning have been traditionally disseminated through single case-studies and clinical reports in the psychodynamic literature. More recently, in a world that rightly demands rigorous evidence that therapeutic approaches work, psychodynamic researchers have risen to the challenge of demonstrating therapeutic effectiveness through outcome research. There is now a body of literature to this effect that includes short and long-term interventions with individuals, groups, and people presenting with different psychological problems. I have listed some of the texts that report these findings in the Bibliography, including a recent meta-analysis (where many studies are pooled and re-analysed) which powerfully demonstrates the effectiveness of psychodynamic interventions. The findings from attachment research are also important in underscoring the utility and efficacy of the psychodynamic approach, particularly with clients who have borderline personality disorder. It is anticipated that increasingly sophisticated neuro-imaging will also highlight the effectiveness of the psychodynamic approach.

The major challenge for psychodynamic practice in recent years has been the demand to prove that our form of counselling is effective and relevant in an age that demands instant results, and when longer-term work can be viewed as unnecessary and of poor value. Funding for psychological treatment in both the public and private spheres now requires that therapeutic effectiveness is demonstrated primarily through symptom reduction, for example a reduction in anxiety symptoms. This poses a challenge for psychodynamic practitioners since symptom reduction on its own has not determined effectiveness in psychodynamic work. Indeed sometimes symptoms reduce only after other psychological changes have been made.

A further challenge comes from the fact that the current 'gold standard' for psychotherapeutic research is the randomized controlled trial (RCT). In RCT research clients are selected because they have a 'pure' presentation of the problem being researched, which means they have straightforward rather than complex difficulties; for example they suffer only from depression, not depression and anxiety. Participants are then randomly assigned to one of two or more conditions, including the psychological approach under investigation plus a control group. The aim of this is to demonstrate that it is the treatment under investigation which has made the difference to their symptoms rather than, for example, the passage of time.

The RCT is designed to be used with manualized therapies, where there are clear guidelines about what to do at each stage of therapy. This means it can be established that all the practitioners are doing the same thing. I suspect you can see for yourself how contrary to most psychodynamic work such a requirement is, since therapy is determined by adherence to a protocol rather than driven by the needs of the client, and there is an underlying assumption that all clients respond to the treatment in the same way. However, the reality in the consulting room is that clients rarely present with the 'uncomplicated' or pure problems that were studied in research trials, so research findings are not necessarily a true guide as to how well real clients will respond to the treatment. Furthermore, the RCT was not devised specifically to measure psychotherapeutic effectiveness, it has been taken from physical medicine, where it is easier to control the variables. For this reason I and others question whether the RCT is the best method of establishing efficacy in any psychological therapy, including CBT. Certainly it should not be the sole way of evaluating therapeutic effectiveness.

But, because we have rarely used the RCT to demonstrate therapeutic effectiveness, the psychodynamic community has been wrongly accused of lacking an evidence base and, worse, of not being effective. This has been hugely frustrating when we do have evidence of therapeutic effectiveness, but that evidence is discounted. In order to ensure that psychodynamic approaches continue to be offered and funded researchers have increasingly felt under pressure to use the RCT, despite the inherent limitations of doing so. For example, an RCT study has just begun using a new manualized short-term psychodynamic therapy – Dynamic Interpersonal Therapy (DIT). It has been developed in London by Alessandra Lemma, Peter Fonagy and Mary Target based on the competency framework established for competent psychodynamic practice. It is this kind of response to the challenges faced by dynamic practitioners that will maintain our position in the therapeutic mainstream.

I have chosen to end this book by looking at the issue of efficacy and the challenges for psychodynamic counselling of the requirement to provide 'scientific evidence' to demonstrate its effectiveness. This is because, although psychodynamic practice is an exciting and evolving approach that is responsive to discoveries in developmental psychology and neuroscience, and has a proven track record, it is under threat as a treatment, particularly in the public sector. In part I think we have only ourselves to blame, since in the past we have been too slow to come out of our consulting rooms and make the case for our approach when it has been challenged. But I also think there are psycho-cultural reasons why psychodynamic approaches have come under threat.

One of these is to do with how, as individuals and as a society, we manage uncertainty and helplessness in the face of the challenges that confront us. We live at a time when we are constantly informed through a 24-hour media of threats to our security and future wellbeing, yet individually we can do little or nothing to change the level of those threats. Consequently, we feel anxious, but unable to do much, leading to increased levels of stress. This includes the larger anxieties about global warming and terrorism as well as personal uncertainty in a fast-changing society. We tend to seek relief from uncertainty and anxiety by externalizing our concerns and attempting to overcome them through certainty and action. The proliferation of protocols and the 'tick-box' culture is evidence of how we try to take ever-tighter control of the world around us in order to achieve that certainty. This fits in well with therapeutic models like CBT, with its active stance and the apparent certainty it offers. By contrast the psychodynamic approach is an uneasy bedfellow since it asks us to explore our anxiety about uncertainty, without taking premature action, and to think rather than act. And, at a time when we look for instant solutions, the psychodynamic approach offers no promise that problems can be resolved easily or quickly.

At the same time Western cultural ideals emphasize the value of independence and autonomy, without proper recognition that these attributes can only be achieved through a satisfactory experience of dependence (ideally in our early lives with our parents). Many people presenting for psychological help have not had that satisfactory experience and lack a sense of an internal secure base. The psychodynamic approach seeks to give them a satisfactory experience of dependence in order for them to internalize it so they can lead more independent lives but also know how to ask for help when they need it in an appropriate way (this is called 'mature dependence'). However, our society abhors the notion of dependence to the extent that some therapies seek to deny that clients have any dependency needs towards their counsellor at all, often in spite of evidence to the contrary. Clients become frightened by the idea of being dependent on a counsellor, fearing loss of what control they have over their lives. The attraction of therapies that offer the promise of change without dependence is understandable in these circumstances.

So how do those of us who value the psychodynamic approach meet these challenges? We need to be still more proactive in coming out from our consulting rooms and demonstrating the effectiveness of our approach. We need to be more vocal in arguing that our ideas are current and relevant; that they are both intellectually robust and based on a series of premises that, at root, are straightforward, understandable and therapeutically valid. We also need to challenge some of the dominant cultural ideals such as the overvaluing of autonomy and being in control, which impact on how both counselling and research are undertaken. Lastly, there is the challenge of demonstrating that psychodynamic ideas are a useful way of understanding the world in which we live and our response to the changes that impact on our lives.

Bibliography

General texts

Jacobs, M. (2006) *The Presenting Past: The Core of Psychodynamic Counselling and Therapy*, 3rd edn. Maidenhead: Open University Press.

Leiper, R. and Maltby, M. (2004) *The Psychodynamic Approach to Therapeutic Change.* London: Sage.

Symington, N. (2006) *A Healing Conversation: How Healing Happens.* London: Karnac.

Skills books

Howard, S. (2010) *Skills in Psychodynamic Counselling and Therapy.* London: Sage.

Jacobs, M. (2010) *Psychodynamic Counselling in Action*, 4th edn. London: Sage.

Lemma, A. (2003) *Introduction to the Practice of Psychoanalytic Psychotherapy.* Chichester: Wiley.

Short-term counselling

Allen, J.G. and Fonagy, P. (eds) (2006) *Handbook of Mentalization-Based Treatment.* Chichester: Wiley.

Coren, A. (2010) *Short-Term Psychotherapy: A Psychodynamic Approach*, 2nd edn. Basingstoke: Palgrave.

Coughlin Della Silva, P. (2004) *Intensive Short-Term Dynamic Psychotherapy: Theory and Technique.* London: Karnac.

Psychodynamic competences

Lemma, A., Roth, A. and Pilling, S. (2008) *The Competencies Required to Deliver Effective Psychoanalytic/Psychodynamic Therapy*. Research Department of Clinical, Educational and Health Psychology, UCL. Available at www.ucl.ac.uk/clinical-psychology/CORE/psychodynamic_framework.htm.

Attachment theory

Bowlby, J. (1988) *A Secure Base: Clinical Applications of Attachment Theory*. London: Routledge.

Holmes, Jeremy (1994) *John Bowlby and Attachment Theory*. London: Routledge.

Holmes, J. (2009) *Exploring in Security: Towards an Attachment-Informed Psychoanalytic Psychotherapy*. London: Routledge.

Psychodynamic theory

Casement, A. (2001) *Carl Gustav Jung*. London: Sage.

Christopher, E. and McFarland Solomon, H. (eds) (2000) *Jungian Thought in the Modern World*. London: Free Association Books.

De Young, P. (2003) *Relational Psychotherapy: A Primer*. New York: Routledge.

Fordham, M. and Hobdell, R. (1998) *Freud, Jung, Klein – The Fenceless Field: Essays on Psychoanalysis and Analytical Psychology*. London: Routledge.

Hinshelwood, R. and Robinson, S. (2003) *Introducing Melanie Klein*. London: Icon Books.

Jacobs, M. (2003) *Sigmund Freud*, 2nd edn. London: Sage.

Jozef Perelberg, R. (ed.) (2005) *Freud: A Modern Reader*. London: Whurr.

Lickierman, M. (2002) *Melanie Klein: Her Work in Context*. London: Continuum.

Mollon, P. (2001) *Releasing the Self: The Healing Legacy of Heinz Kohut*. London: Whurr.

Phillips, A. (2007) *Winnicott*. London: Penguin.

Symington, N. (1986) *The Analytic Experience: Lectures from the Tavistock*. London: Free Association Books.

Neuroscience

Gerhardt, S. (2004) *Why Love Matters: How Affection Shapes a Baby's Brain*. Hove: Brunner-Routledge.

Hart, S. (2008) *Brain, Attachment, Personality: An Introduction to Neuroaffective Development*. London: Karnac Books.

Solms, M. and Turnbull, O. (2002) *The Brain and the Inner World: An Introduction to the Neuroscience of Subjective Experience*. London: Karnac.

Supervision

Driver, C. and Martin, E. (eds) (2005) *Supervision and the Analytic Attitude*. London: Whurr.

Hawkins, P. and Shohet, R. (2006) *Supervision in the Helping Professions*, 3rd edn. Buckingham: Open University Press.

The Health Professions Council (HPC) website: www.hpc-uk.org

Petts, A. and Shapley, B. (eds) (2007) *On Supervision: Psychoanalytic and Jungian Perspectives*. London: Karnac.

Research in psychodynamic approaches

Cooper, M. (2008) *Essential Research Findings in Counselling and Psychotherapy: The Facts are Friendly*. London: Sage.

Leuzinger-Bohleber, M. and Target, M. (2002) *Outcomes of Psychoanalytic Treatment: Perspectives for Therapists and Researchers.* London: Whurr.

Levy, R. and Ablon, J.S. (eds) (2009) *Handbook of Evidence-Based Psychodynamic Psychotherapy: Bridging the Gap Between Science and Practice.* Berlin: Springer-Verlag.

Shedler, J. (2010) 'The efficacy of psychodynamic psychotherapy', *American Psychologist,* 65: 98–109.

Psychodynamic approaches and society

Gerhardt, S. (2010) *The Selfish Society: How We All Forgot to Love One Another and Made Money Instead.* London: Harper Collins.

Lemma, A. and Patrick, M. (eds) (2010) *Off the Couch: Contemporary Psychoanalytic Applications.* London: Routledge.

Index

analytic ear 75
analytical psychology 36
archetypes 39
assessment phase 5, 68
attachment crisis 64
attachment theory 30, 49–52
attention, evenly suspended 73–5

baby *see* mother–baby
behaviour
    instinctive 18–19
    unconsciously motivated 12–13
boundaries 59, 60
Bowlby, J. 30, 41
    and attachment theory 49–52
British Association of Counselling
    (BACP) 94, 95

change, psychological 4
    importance of therapeutic
        relationship 22–5
    resistance to 25–6
character *see* personality
child time 84
childhood experiences 18, 19–22
    see also personality development
Children Act 96
client–counsellor relationship *see*
    therapeutic relationship
collective unconscious 38–9
comforter 48
complexes 40
confidentiality 95–6
conflicting emotions/desires 13–14
conscience 32
conscious mind 8, 12, 31
    and conflicts 14
    conscious awareness 9
    hiding uncomfortable truths from
        12–13
containment concept 46
Controversial Discussions 29
couch, use of 92
counselling
    approaches compared 88–93
    see also psychodynamic
        counselling
counselling skills *see* skills
counsellor
    challenges and rewards 93–4
    reasons for becoming 86–7
    see also personal counselling;
        supervision
countertransference 22–5
    as advanced empathy 65–7
    and interpretation 82
CPD *see* personal counselling;
    supervision

Data Protection Act 95–6
death instinct 42, 47
defences, psychological
    14–17, 33
denial 15
dependency 48–9, 103
depressive position 43–5
development theory *see* personality
    development

dreams 9–11, 32, 36, 68, 78–9
Dynamic Interpersonal Therapy 102

ego 21, 31–3
   of developing infant 47
ego-ideal 32
electra conflict 34, 35
empathy 66
ending therapy 69–70, 94, 98–9
envy 42
episodic memory 20–1
ethical practice 94–6
evenly suspended attention 73–5
extroversion 36, 37, 38

false self concept 48
fantasy 20, 43, 47, 62–3, 63–4
feeling function 37
first session 1–3, 4, 57–8, 64
Fonagy, P. 50
Fordham, M. 40–1
formality 51–2
free association 67–8
Freud, S. 7, 27–8
   development theory 33–5
   and dreams 36
   models of the mind 30–3
   and sexual instincts 19, 28, 33
   views on unconscious mind 8–9, 10, 11, 67

Health Professions Council 96
holding environment 58–61
hysteria 27

id, the 31–2
implicit memory 21
Independents, the 29–30
infantile amnesia 20

informed consent 4–5, 72–3
inner world 3, 8–9
   dynamic nature of 12–13
   inner conflict 13–14
instincts 13, 18–19
interpretation 79–83
introversion 36, 37, 38
intuition 37

John's story
   dreams 10
   end of counselling 98–9
   hospital/illness fantasy 62–3
   late arrival and holiday arrangements 77
   referral and first meeting 1–3, 4
   transference and countertransference 23–4, 66, 68, 69, 82
   and waiting room changes 83
jokes 11
Jung, C. 7, 28, 29
   collective and personal unconscious 38–9
   complexes 40
   models of the psyche 35–8

key concepts *see* psychodynamic model
Klein, M. 29, 41–3
   development theory 43–6

late arrival 60–1, 76–7
listening skills 73–6

memory systems 20–1
Mentalization-Based Treatment 41, 50
mind, the
   Freud's model 30–3
   Jung's model 36–40

mother–baby relationship 46–9
    attachment theory 49–52
motivation
    instinctive behaviour 18–19
    unconscious sources 12–13

neuroscience 53–6
neutrality, therapeutic 61–3

Object Relations School 30, 46
objects and object relationships 11–12
    and change 22
    transference and the counsellor 64, 79–80
Oedipus complex 34, 35, 45

paranoid-schizoid position 43–5
personal counselling 65, 84, 85–6, 87–8
personality development 19–22
    Bowlby's attachment theory 49–52
    Freud's theory 28, 33–5
    Klein's theory 43–6
    Winnicott's ideas 46–9
practical skill *see* skills
preconscious awareness 14
preconscious mind 31
primary self 40–1
privacy 59–60
professional development *see* personal counselling; supervision
projection 16–17
psyche, the 36–8
psychoanalysis 7–8, 28
    see also psychotherapy
psychodynamic counselling
    benefits and risks of 99–100
    challenges to 102–4

psychodynamic counselling *cont.*
    efficacy of 98–102
    other approaches compared 88–91
    psychotherapy *vs* counselling 91–3
    stages of 68–70
psychodynamic model, overview of 3, 7–8
    current developments 52–6
    inner world/unconscious processes 8–12
        inner conflict 13–14
    instincts 13, 18–19
    personality and childhood experiences 19–22
    psychological defences 14–17
    psychological symptoms 17–18
    role of therapeutic relationship 22–6
psychological change *see* change
psychological turbulence 13
psychological type 38
psychosexual development 33–5
psychotherapy 91–3

randomized controlled trials 101–2
rationalization 15
record keeping 95
relationships 5–6, 13
    and survival 19
    see also therapeutic relationship
repression 28, 31
research 100

safe environment 58–61
Seduction Theory 27–8
self, development of 21, 40–1
    see also personality development
sensation function 37

sessions
  first 1–3, 4, 57–8, 64
  length of 60
  session notes 95
  structure of 67, 83–4
  see also ending therapy
sexual drive/instincts 19, 28, 31
  and Freud's theory of
    development 33–5
shadow identity 38
short-term therapy 90
skills, counselling 71–2
  developing evenly suspended
    attention 73–5
  gaining informed consent 72–3
  listening to unconscious
    communication 75–9
  making interpretations 79–83
  structuring sessions 83–4
slips of the tongue 11, 32
splitting 17
stages of counselling
  beginning 68–9
  middle 69
  ending 69–70, 94, 98–9
  see also first session
Stern, D. 50
superego 31–3
supervision 67, 91–2, 96–8
symptoms, psychological 17–18
  symptom relief 89–90, 100–1
synchronicity 39

therapeutic effectiveness 98–104
therapeutic relationship 3–4, 5
  central role of 22–5
  at different stages 68–70
  safe place and boundaries
    58–61
  therapeutic neutrality 61–3
  see also transference relationship
thinking function 37
trainees 65, 80, 91–2
  see also personal counselling;
    supervision
transference relationship 22–5, 48–9,
    63–4, 69
  counsellor as object 62, 79–80
  impact on counsellor 64–5
  and interpretation 81
  using countertransference 22–3,
    24, 65–7
transitional object 48
Triangle of Person 81
turbulence, psychological 13

unconscious mind 8–9, 31
  Freud's concept 28
  gaining access to 67–8
  Jung's concepts 38–9
  listening to unconscious
    communication 75–9
  see also inner world

Winnicott, D. 30, 41, 46–9